The Labyrinth in Culture and Society

The *Labyrinth* in *Culture* and *Society*

PATHWAYS TO WISDOM

Jacques Attali

translated by
Joseph Rowe

North Atlantic Books
Berkeley, California

Published by
North Atlantic Books
P.O. Box 12327
Berkeley, California 94712

Labyrinth image courtesy Veriditas, the Worldwide Labyrinth Project,
www.gracecathedral.org. Background image based on illustration #81.
Cover and book design by Legacy Media.
Printed in the United States of America.

The Labyrinth in Culture and Society: Pathways to Wisdom is sponsored
by the Society for the Study of Native Arts and Sciences, a nonprofit educational corporation whose goals are to develop an educational and crosscultural perspective linking various scientific, social, and artistic fields; to
nurture a holistic view of arts, sciences, humanities, and healing; and to
publish and distribute literature on the relationship of mind, body, and
nature.

Library of Congress Cataloging-in-Publication Data

Attali, Jacques.
  [Chemins de sagesse. English]
  The labyrinth in culture and society : pathways to wisdom /
Jacques Attali.
     p.   cm
  ISBN 1-55643-265-8 (pbk.)
     1. Labyinths—Religious aspects—Psychology.   2. Spiritual life.
3. Labyrinths—Psychological aspects.   4. Conduct of life.   I. Title.
  BL325.L3A8713   1998
  291.3'7—dc21   97-49276
                                                                    CIP

1 2 3 4 5 6 7 8 9 / 03 02 01 00 99

Contents

Preface

*"We must relearn labyrinthine thinking and restudy
the strategies necessary for our evolution towards
a reinvention of the secrets of this ancient wisdom."*
—Jacques Attali

What does a renowned French intellectual, who is an economic theorist, an author of twenty-five books, and a scholar
who studies the main trends in human history to use them to
forecast the future, have in common with an American female
Episcopal priest, who is an author and a transpersonal psychotherapist? Labyrinths, of course. And this goes straight to the
heart of the matter before us.

Labyrinths are ancient patterns that galvanize the human psyche toward unity and wholeness. And no one articulates this better then Jacques Attali.

Vast change is shaking the roots of Western Civilization. What
we assumed in the past to be permanent and unchangeable has
become vulnerable to the global mind change sweeping the planet. Like palm trees struggling against high winds, our institutions
that have served as the backbone of our culture are bending to
the point of breaking. We are in a full scale shakedown process
and ready or not, ideas that have served as the cornerstone of
who we think we are, are outmoded and falling by the wayside.

Westerners are confronted with sharp learning curves especially within the technological revolution. Individuals are chal-
lenged to learn new skills—mastering the VCR was the first one,
then keeping up with the generations of computer hardware and
software, and now designing a Home page and learning to surf
the internet—to name a few major ones. The terms upgrade, e-
mail, Web site and download has forced their way into our

vocabulary. Institutions are in an even more challenging situation. First they need to know how to use these technological advancements to get their message out. Second, these advancements are changing the hard wiring of the human psyche and therefore institutions need radically to change the way they think about what they are offering to society in order to navigate their paths into the future. As in any process of change, much must be given up. We must relinquish our linear thinking and single-task focus as we shift our vision to embrace nonlinear processes, multi-tasking, and networking modes of thinking.

This is where Jacques Attali makes a major contribution. He senses how Western culture needs to reinvent itself in order to further the heart and soul of humanity. Labyrinths serve as "symbols, the basis of myth and as subliminal communications," states Attali, and out of this comes a network of connections—people to people, person to institution, institution to institution and institution to society.

Attali offers a historical analysis of how we elected, over the centuries, to rid ourselves of the indirect path for the supposed superiority of the straight line. We moved from the meandering to the linear, from the complex to the singular, from the curved and sensualto the straight and narrow. Consequently our thinking became shallow and unable to grasp the depth of meaning the labyrinthine symbolic world held for us. Now, as we enter the twenty-first century, this daedal depth of wisdom is recapturing our imaginations. The complex patterns enfolded with these ancient designs are calling us to reclaim the lost and forgotten parts of ourselves. In responding to this call we will develop a richer culture. In fact, now more than ever, we have the potential to create one. Through his concept of a "new nomadism" explicated in this work, Attali characterizes the nature of this future civilization.

Labyrinths are being created all over the Western world. Hospitals are using them in their complementary healing programs, spas are using them for stress reduction, retirements centers are using them for exercise and community building, memorial parks invite their grieving clients to walk to release fears and find solace, churches and cathedrals are using them to quicken the spirit and enliven the religious imagination as parishioners walk the Path of Life.

Inherent in any discussion of labyrinths is a confusing element of definition embedded in the English language. The two etymologies—labyrinth (from the Greek *labrus,* "double axe" and maze (from the Old English *mazen,* "to bewilder")—are often used interchangeably. On the metaphoric level, as Dr. Attali uses these words, this is acceptable. However, a confusion arises if one intends physically to walk a labyrinth or a maze. Insofar as these are experientially opposite to each other false expectations from the one can muddle or distort the event of the other.

A labyrinth is uni-cursal, meaning, "one path." It has no cul-de-sacs or dead ends and is in truth designed for the walker to find his or her way to the center. Mazes, on the other hand, are multi-cursal. They comprise many entrances that create multiple paths fraught with cul-de-sacs and dead-ends.

Mazes are often seen as games and are created in order to have the walker lose his or her way. Although some people consider the labyrinth a single-path maze, this subdefinition itself does not clarify the confusion people may encounter. The author, for instance, defines each artifact thoroughly in the beginning of his work and then—as he moves to the rich symbolic and metaphoric level—he artfully allows the definition between the two to blur, and he uses "labyrinth" as a special category whose meaning he develops. For instance, he describes the internet as a labyrinth to make his point about the recovery of labyrinthine thinking.

The Labyrinth in Culture and Society is an adventure in reading. It contains a thorough historical documentation of the labyrinth down through the ages; it also provides a crosscultural prospective. Attali not only uncovers the roots of these ancient patterns, he also examines them in the light of our present cultural upheaval. Through this examination he encourages a fresh, yet ancient, perspective to take root in our modern-day search for a new understanding of ourselves.

Enjoy!

The Reverend Dr. Lauren Artress,
author of *Walking a Sacred Path:*
Rediscovering the Labyrinth as a
Spiritual Tool

Acknowledgments

I would like to express special thanks to Jeanne Auzenet, to Frédérique Jourdaa, and to Josseline Rivière for their contributions to the documentation and illustrations of this book.

Introduction

Four Stories as a Beginning

Doom

In a distant future era, cannibal phantoms have invaded the Earth. Annihilating armies and slaughtering whole nations, they have destroyed or enslaved every form of life they have encountered. The Earth has become its own hell.

One remaining rebel fighter desperately assembles a ragged band of surviving comrades, and they board their only intact spaceship and fly to a distant orbital station. Once at the station, they hope to rebuild their forces and prepare the reconquest of the Earth. In order to obtain the devices that can save them, they must travel through winding corridors strewn with traps, dead ends, insoluble labyrinths, explosive drums, pits with impaling stakes, radioactive debris, and ceilings that descend and crush. These labyrinths were constructed long ago in order to protect the precious rockets from invaders. The tragic irony is that the maze's original purpose of protecting humankind from possible invaders has now become the deadliest of enemies for these fugitives of space.

The phantoms are also in pursuit of the rebel band. Captured stragglers are transformed into cannibal mutants, hallucinatory specters, lost souls, pallid haunting ghouls, spirits of pain, insane cyber-demons, and soldiers of hell.

In order to get through the labyrinth, the rebel fighters must discover the keys and codes of various barriers, neutralize force-fields, unlock lethal machines, disable the ceilings, detect secret passageways, avoid dead ends, and destroy the phantoms before they seize and transform them into evil allies. To help in this mission, they possess the most sophisticated weapons and the most advanced scrambling and camouflage devices. But above all, there are courage, perseverance, keen memory, curiosity, shrewdness, physical reflexes, and intuition.

Such are the premises of Doom, one of the most successful video games ever. In it, the player sitting at the console identifies with this rebel fighter, choosing weapons and routes, running through the labyrinth of death, and completing a veritable marathon of killings in the process—a *slugathon,* as it is so cutely termed—before having a chance to win the road to escape and survival.

Chartres

When medieval pilgrims took to the road from Paris to Compostela, they had to cross the great prairie of the Beauce. Finally, they beheld the grandeur and serenity of the nave of Chartres cathedral looming up from the plains around them, one of the first of those extravagant prayers in stone of the late Middle Ages. At this moment, they must surely have felt that they would undergo an essential mystical experience there. When they later arrived before the western facade of the most luminous basilica ever built by human hands, the highest Romanesque tower ever erected to the glory of God, they might first admire a sublime circular stained-glass window directly above the entry porch, which depicts the splendor of the Most High (see illustration #34).[*]

As they penetrated into the interior of this immense vessel of stone and light, wrought through the agency of the mysterious Écarlate, they discovered something remarkable at their feet, covering the floor of the nave from the third to the sixth bay: a strange circular stonework design of the exact same dimensions as the stained-glass window high above them on the western wall.[72]

Around the perimeter of the circle, there are 113 scallops, or

---

[*] [Translator's note] The author uses the French word "dédale" here, which is usually translated as "maze." The distinction he makes between it and the labyrinth does not correspond to the one that is current in English.

cusps and foils, called lunations, engraved with the verses of the Miserere.[88] Inside the circle, this labyrinth is composed of eleven elongated concentric loops, separated by a band of black stone demarcating the brown quarry-stone path that comprises the entire floor of the cathedral. There are no wrong turns possible in this labyrinth, yet the center is always farthest just when one feels it is about to be attained.

At the entrance to the well-worn brown stone path of the labyrinth, the pilgrim kneels long in prayer. Then he or she embarks upon this recapitulation of the perilous path of the mortal on the way to Paradise, of the pilgrim in search of the inaccessible Jerusalem, of the sinner traveling towards salvation. Winding its way through to the fifth loop, which borders the center, the path then moves slowly away from it and back towards it again, changing directions six times, ultimately passing through 370 hairpin turns, walking a total distance that calculates to precisely ten times the height of the nave.[72] The goal at the center is a large six-petalled rosette, itself a replica of the shape formed by the sunlight shining through the stained-glass window. At the rosette's center is an engraved copper plaque that bears the image of Theseus, Ariadne, and the Minotaur.

This is a strange road, equidistant between the summit of the cathedral's vault and the water in the underground river running beneath it. On the day of the summer solstice, it becomes a vibrational vortex, for the solstice is a fundamental reference point in the secret architecture of this most cosmic of God's vessels.

Australia

In a desolate land in the heart of the harsh desert that covers central Australia, ancient aborigine sages like to tell the story of the creation of the world, when two sisters of the Wagilag clan had incestuous relations with men from their kinship line.[43] As punishment for flouting this major prohibition, they were expelled from their land and condemned to wander endlessly with their children and possessions through the burning sands.

Year after year they roamed aimlessly, lost in the void of an existence without goal. They discovered animals, plants, and previously unknown lands, which they named and thereby caused to be born. One evening they halted, completely exhausted, near the pond of Mirrarrmina in the country of Liyagalawumirri. They made camp there for the night, unaware of the fact that this was the home of Wititj, one of the terrible sacred pythons. Dizzy with fatigue and distress, they built a hut out of bark and began to prepare their meal when the python, enraged by this invasion of his territory, sucked up all the water of the nearby pond and spewed it out onto the trespassers. Thus the first monsoon was born. In a panic, the two exiled sisters and their troupe of ragamuffins took shelter inside their flimsy hut, singing and dancing so as to turn away the rain and thunder. But to no avail: the waters continued to mount, soon covering the entire surface of the earth. Still thirsting for revenge, the python Wititj swallowed the two women and their children. But the other sacred pythons found this vengeance excessive and persuaded Wititj to renounce it, whereupon the serpent vomited out the women and children and blew the water away with a great breath. Exhausted from all this effort, Wititj then collapsed in a faint, imprinting the form of his body onto the soil, which traced out a labyrinth pattern that is still visible today. In a vain attempt to flee this inhospitable region, the women then became lost in the coils of this living labyrinth. Regaining consciousness, Wititj was furious to find them still there, wandering among his coils. Going back on his promise to his brothers, Wititj swallowed the little band once more. This time he would only consent to vomit out two enormous boulders, which still stand not far from the pond of Mirrarrmina (see illustration #69).[43]

In their songs and dances today, the Australian aborigines still tell the edifying story of the two ill-fated women and their living labyrinth. It serves to remind humans of all times and places, also expelled from paradise for violation of a taboo, that the quest for the Promised Land demands not only the courage to travel through deserts but the will to enter labyrinths, where there is a hope of finding the path of redemption even when it is said to be closed to sinners.

Crete

The forgotten son of the union of Zeus, God of gods, with Europa, "dark" daughter of the Phoenician ruler Agenor, Minos was adopted by his stepfather Astericus, king of Crete. Succeeding to the throne in his own turn, Minos married the dazzling Pasiphaë, who bore him four daughters (Ariadne, Phaedra, Akakallis, Xenodike) and four sons (Glaukos, Katreus, Deukalion, Androgeos).[46]

Life was peaceful in the palace of Knossos as long as Minos was able to fulfill the demand of Zeus's brother Poseidon, god of the sea, upon whom the island's prosperity depended. Every year, he demanded a sacrifice of ever more magnificent bulls (see illustration #24). A time arrived when Minos could no longer find sufficiently worthy sacrificial beasts on any of the islands, and he asked Poseidon to furnish the victim himself. In answer to his prayer, the god caused the waves to bring forth a bull upon the beach—a bull so imposing, so splendid and immaculate, that Minos had not the heart to sacrifice him. Furious at this ingratitude, Poseidon decided to avenge himself upon the unfaithful king by taking possession of that which was dearest to him. Incarnating himself in the animal that he had just created, the god of the sea charmed Pasiphaë, the king's wife. Completely seduced, she decided to give herself to the bull. She hired the services of a strange Greek craftsman named Daedalus, inventor of the carpenter's square. He had taken refuge at Knossos, fleeing from Athens after murdering his brilliant student Talos, for having stolen his inventions of the compass and the saw. In order to satisfy the adulterous queen, this clever criminal designed a leather cow into which Pasiphaë could climb and hide herself. Poseidon then made love to the wife of his enemy. From this union was born a creature with human body and the head of a bull, who was named the Minotaur (see illustration #23). When

King Minos learned of his existence, he refrained from punishing the queen, so as to avoid scandal—or perhaps he realized that this affliction had its origin in his own apostasy. Since there were no prisons as yet in this land, Minos had this same Daedalus construct a monumental labyrinth, modeled on the tomb of the Egyptian pharaoh Menes, who had just had himself buried inside a maze of winding corridors.

At this time, another misfortune befell King Minos—his son Androgeos was killed in Athens, at that time a tributary city of the great Cretan power. And he was killed by a bull. In reprisal, Minos demanded that the Athenian King Aegeus deliver seven young men and seven young women to Crete, once every nine years. The Cretan king sent these sacrificial victims into the labyrinth, where the half-human, half-bull Minotaur would avenge this murder of a man by a bull, by tearing the youths to pieces.

On the eve of the third sacrificial meal, Theseus, a long-lost son of the king of Athens, decided to deliver himself voluntarily to the monster, in an attempt to kill him and put an end to this bloody form of tribute. He promised his father Aegeus that if he were to return safely, his ship would hoist a white sail on its mast.

Hardly had he arrived in Crete, along with the thirteen other young Athenians selected for sacrifice, when Theseus seduced Ariadne, daughter of Minos and Pasiphaë. This young princess also had access to the counsel of Daedalus, and she provided her lover with a magical thread that would guide him through the labyrinth, together with a ball of wax that he was to throw into the Minotaur's mouth. Thus equipped, Theseus ventured deep into the labyrinth, slew the monster, and came out again alive, rewinding the magical thread as he returned. He also saved the lives of the chosen victims, thereby violating the sacrificial pact signed by Athens. Acting swiftly to avoid Minos, who was enraged at being robbed of his retribution, he then escaped by sea, setting sail with Ariadne, her younger sister Phaedra, and the other Athenians. On the island of Naxos, safe from the troubles he had left behind, Theseus seduced Phaedra and abandoned Ariadne to the god Dionysos, who consoled her by transforming her into a constellation of stars. Sailing shortly afterward to the island of Delos, Theseus celebrated his freedom by inventing the dance—at once a tracing of a path, a procession, and a trance—which was inspired by his conquest of the labyrinth.

Satiated with all his feasting and glory, Theseus sailed back to Athens. But he had forgotten his promise to his father to hoist a white sail on his mast. Seeing the black sails on the horizon, Aegeus despaired and threw himself into the sea that still bears his name. Meanwhile, the angry Cretan king had settled upon Daedalus as the man responsible for all these disasters, because of the help he had given to Pasiphaë and Poseidon, as well as to Ariadne and Theseus. He imprisoned the Athenian, along with his son Icarus, inside the labyrinth of his own making. The blind alleys there were so complex that even these two artisans could not find their way out. But Daedalus was never in lack of schemes and techniques, and the master craftsman fashioned wings out of feathers and wax, which he and his son fixed to their shoulders. Before they took off, he warned Icarus to fly neither too high, because of the wax that could melt in the heat of the sun, nor too low, because of the feathers, which could become wet and heavy with water from the mists. Intoxicated by his ascent, the young man flew so high that he lost his wings and plunged to drown in the sea before his father's eyes.

Pursued by the Cretans and haunted by a sense of responsibility for the deaths of both Icarus and Talos, Daedalus began a long, wandering voyage—a kind of labyrinthine flight of the fugitive—from island to island across the Mediterranean. Frustrated by his failure to track Daedalus down (despite numerous forays of pursuit of him), Minos hit upon a cunning ruse: over the entire Mediterranean world, he let it be known that a great reward was to be had by anyone who could find a way to pass a silken thread through all the spiral turns of a conch shell. Daedalus got word of this challenge on the Sicilian island of Cernicos, where he had found refuge. He could not resist the temptation to propose a solution anonymously—this he accomplished by attaching the thread to an ant and pouring honey into the interior. When Minos heard of the solution, he was certain that only the brilliant Athenian engineer could have been the origin of it, and rushed to the island to punish him. But the Sicilians protected their guest, and got rid of Minos by pouring boiling water into his bath.

Meanwhile, the ingrate Theseus was spending many happy days with Phaedra, second daughter of Minos. But misfortune arrived when she fell in love with her stepson, Hippolytus. Poseidon, taking the form of a tidal wave, killed Hippolytus in revenge for the murder of his own son, the Minotaur, and Phaedra committed suicide. Theseus married for the third time, this time to Medea, who sent him to visit Hades, from which he returned. Ultimately, weary of everything, he withdrew to Skyros where he was killed by King Lysiamedes.

This sublime epic, one of the most popular stories of antiquity, was heard on all the great roads of the Balkans, where countless minstrels and wandering bards earned their bread by chanting it. When written literature and theater began to appear, it inspired poems and plays.[114] Sophocles wrote his *Daidalos,* as did Aristophanes and Philip of Euboulos. There is a *Theseus and the Cretans* by Euripedes, as well as by Aristophanes and Sophocles. Both Antiphanes and Alexis wrote a *Minos,* and Alceus a *Pasiphaë.* The word *labyrinth* became common, as did the word *daidalos,* which was used as an equivalent in Greek. It appears thirty-three times in Homer, eight in Hesiod.[114]

Legendary figures naturally elude historical research, and there are no grounds for certainty as to whether the events of this legend had any real basis.

There is even uncertainty as to the origin of the word "labyrinth" itself, which remains an etymological mystery today. Herodotus, using it much later, admitted that he did not know its origin.[66] Linguists have held that the word came from *labrys,* which designated the Lydian double axe emblem of Cretan kings, representing the waxing and waning moons, a symbol of the creative and destructive power of the God-King. According to other authors, the word's roots are neither Cretan nor Greek, and come from the Lydian term for axe, or the Lycian term for cavern.[141] But there is yet another Greek etymology that has been proposed, designating the movements of a fish caught in a trap.[114] Early in the twentieth century, the archeologist Sir Arthur Evans discovered a tablet in the ruins of the palace of Minos at Knossos, dating from 1300 B.C., on which a word was engraved that designated the palace, whose pronunciation would sound something like: *Da-pu-ri-to*. Finally, in Greek, *daidalos* means a work of art, and another synonym, *Meandros*, was also the name of a Greek king who committed suicide by plunging into a river for having vowed to cut his son's throat if he were victorious.[113]

The only incontestable reality that emerges from all these contradictory versions is the power of the myth itself. Theseus forever remains one of the most complex heroes of Western civilization, and his passage through the labyrinth one of the most beautiful of human voyages.

Labyrinths Everywhere

In these four stories, which come to us from four radically different directions of space-time and myth, we find some of the constant themes of human history: misdeed as a cause of exile, prison as a protection, wandering as initiation, shadows as a threat, vanity engendering loss, human power in animal form, and, at the end of the road, the Promised Land as the resolution of anguish. These tales also contain certain essential archetypes of human destiny: a being weakened and condemned for having violated rules necessary to collective life, the man of knowledge who brings about changes to human life, the young woman who is able to seduce and console the hero.

And everywhere, typically when one expects it the least, the labyrinth appears. The player of Doom, the pilgrim at Chartres, the aboriginal sisters, and the Cretan hero must all pass through it in order to survive. It is the underlying theme that unifies all these narratives, the path of wisdom that serves as conduit for the message common to all these enigmas—the secret of life.

A Coded Message

For many years, I have been engaged in an effort to uncover signs of the most distant future in some of the least accessible stigmata of the past. The more these studies progress, the more they convince me that everything in our psychic and social make-up today—as well as everything in our self-created human future—draws its inspiration from the imagination of those eighty billion human beings who preceded us on this planet over the last three million years. Among the many signs that they have left for us in such a myriad of ways, the labyrinth is one of the most important. Though one of the most haunting and universal of symbols, it has also been one of the least clearly interpreted.

Is it a mere game, or an essential rite? A work of art, or a mystical guide? A prison, or a doorway to heaven? A place of eternal wandering, or the true road of Paradise? A place of initiation or a reflection of ignorance? Is its purpose to punish us or to heal us? Does it lead to sin or to salvation? And does it represent a very primitive form of writing, or is it a particularly refined mode of symbolic expression?

A mirror in which every civilization can descry its own fantasies, the labyrinth is all of the above. But the sense of it that I wish to emphasize is the labyrinth as a last message transmitted from collective nomadic to sedentary peoples. It is as if they had foreseen that their distant descendants would someday return involuntarily to a nomadic existence, and might be able to rediscover in these forgotten designs a wisdom necessary for the future.

For the labyrinth is more than a design: it is a message. This goes against our cultural presumptions, which make it difficult for us to see how an idea, to say nothing of a philosophy, could be expressed by simple graffiti. In our arrogance, we see only a clumsy tracing, perhaps connected with some sort of game—at best the simpleminded record of a primitive thought-process, at worst a childish scribble.

It would be a serious error to give credence to such overconfident views.

"One picture is worth a thousand words," as Sun Xi wrote in the fifth century, in full knowledge of the Chinese ideograms. Pictures spoke to people long before writing began. They spoke of things of a complexity that has been forgotten by our impoverished alphabets. The labyrinth has always been the master-pattern of dreams where people have drawn upon a fluid syntax far more ancient than the convolutions of language. To whomever can decipher it, paths of wisdom are revealed therein. It teaches human beings to behold their destiny in one glance, as one holds a wounded bird in the palm of one's hand. It enables them constantly to plumb the depths of their own secrets—and to remember them in order to live.

The labyrinth never signifies trivial purposes. One of the most ancient emblems of human thought, it appears where primordial dramas unfold. In those most distant epochs—and not just among Greeks and Australian aborigines—it was already employed as the best way to symbolize complexity, to represent the tragic destiny of inescapable time, and also to prevent profaners from approaching a sanctuary or a tomb. It is a sort of combination of crypt, code of thought, and rite of passage.

Most surprising to me is how we could have overlooked for so long the fact that the ancient ubiquity of the labyrinth has to indicate some fundamental significance, even a major theme of religious history. As we shall see further on in this book, this omission is no doubt related to a fundamental bias of our civilization, which rejects sinuous obscurity and occultation in favor of the straight line, transparence, and simplicity.

I must emphasize that the labyrinth can never be reduced to some sort of local epiphenomenon. We find it occurring everywhere over thousands of years. Amazingly similar patterns recur in stone engravings and painted walls thousands of miles apart, in Scandinavia, Russia, India, Tibet, Greece, Brittany, and in

Africa and America (see illustrations #5 through #20).[14] In the grand scale of things, it is only recently that nomadic ways of life gave way to sedentary ones, and we subsequently find the labyrinth appearing in certain consecrated places, where it symbolizes even the sacred itself. In Egypt, it represented the path taken by the soul. Elsewhere around the Mediterranean, it served as a template for ritual dances. In the later cultures of China and America, it represented the inner voyage of the quest for one's own truth. With the advent of the Crusades in Christianity, it became an elegant and inexpensive means for the faithful to perform a symbolic pilgrimage, wending their way along the lines of a stone labyrinth whose center symbolized Jerusalem (see illustrations #35 through #44). The labyrinth was a generic, implicit indicator of profundity, complexity, and the riddle of human destiny.

And then came the Age of Reason, with its exaltation of transparency and the straight line. From here on, the labyrinth became an enemy, an example of obscurity to be clarified and banished. Efficiency requires going quickly and straightforwardly, so as to save time and to maintain visibility and predictability. Here, the labyrinth disappears as governance, only to reappear (likewise recalling the demise of nomadism) in the sanctuary of garden ornaments, and then in salons as a variety of board games and children's amusements, a number of which are still popular today.

Its exile to mere ornamentation has lasted as long as the industrial revolution. Now this exile is over, and the governing labyrinth has returned. Cities are regaining their labyrinthine qualities. When we look at new market economies, networks of power and influence, diagrams of business and governmental organizations, university curricula, or personal careers, we find them no longer guided solely by the image of the straight line. We instead find a succession of convolutions, traps, dead ends, wrong paths, and jealously guarded sanctums. Wealth and power are henceforth to be found within the terminus of a labyrinth. Computer science itself confirms this image: labyrinthine networks of microprocessors and chips, and the very programs themselves, whose binary instructions are an incessant series of forking paths and choices between them. Video games are also labyrinths to be run, unraveled while avoiding the many traps they hold in store; recently, versions of these games allow Internet uplinks, so that one can play against a multitude of distant partners. The applications of such labyrinths of labyrinths go far beyond games, and will soon form a planetary communication network including all libraries and all memories.

If the planet is thus destined to become an ecolabyrinth, it is certain that each human being already is one. Brain, ears, viscera, nervous system, fingerprints, reproductive code—virtually everything about us can be derived in this way from the genes within a single cell. The journey through this labyrinth leads to embodiment. Modern psychoanalysis forsook the values of rectitude and transparency and revealed the unconscious, crouched like a monster (or a genie) at the end of a labyrinth, arrived at through a scrutiny of the pathways of dreams, with their own mazes replete with forbidden areas, displaced misdirections, and mirrored simulacra. Finally, our literature and entertainment, whether myth or novel, children's fairy-tale or video game, from the most Hermetic poetry to the latest popular movie, can be summarized as Quests, voyages winding their way through tattered trails full of obstacles.

Thinking the Labyrinth

What is the urgency that this subject seems to have for us today? Is it because my own life is like a labyrinth, with blind alleys, and about-faces, where I often discover that I am furthest from the center just when I believe I have found it? Perhaps— but it is equally much more than this, for our cultural as well as our personal identity rests upon a labyrinth. Whether as a stationary pilgrim in a monastery or a player of the video game Doom, human beings today are in the process of becoming virtual nomads: working and shopping at home, navigating without a guide through networks of information and power, with fantasies of belonging to that future elite of deluxe nomads who migrate from pleasure to pleasure, creating all the networks that will soon impose their values on the rest of the planet.

Understanding labyrinths will soon become essential to a mastery of the modern condition.

This is why we must set aside rectitude and transparency: the real world is simply not that way. It is fractal and algebraic, ruled not by symmetries or geometric certitudes. We must relearn labyrinthine thinking and restudy the strategies necessary for our evolution towards a reinvention of the secrets of this ancient wisdom. Myths have much to teach us here. And the first of these, because apparently the closest to us, is that of the Cretan king who made use of a labyrinth so as to dissimulate his barbarity.

But who will be tomorrow's Minos? What power will be able to hide its monstrosity away at the end of a labyrinth? And who will be the Theseus attempting to destroy that power? And who Ariadne, the rebel who reveals the deadly secret to the man she loves? What of Daedalus, the criminal genius looking always for riddles to solve, yet incapable of seeing through his own traps? And the Minotaur, chimera, and barbarous monster, the unconscious enemy implanted in every person, which can be diminished only by its exposure to the light of day? Who is the audacious future Icarus, who will perish from overconfidence in others' talents? And finally, what invention or technology will it be that takes on the role of the wax, signifying both greatness and limitation of human intelligence? Does something dwell unmarked in our midst, or lie disguised in our future, that allows (or will allow) Icarus to fix the wings to his shoulders, thereby offering him an upward escape from his condition—but only on condition that he not come too close to the sun?

From Daedalus to the Internet.... A very long way? Yet a very short way as well: exactly like two neighboring points in a labyrinth.

Daedalus and His Meanderings

One thing needs to be clarified at the start: what does

"labyrinth" designate today? A labyrinth is a complex path, limited by walls, with at least one entrance into a passage leading towards a center or exit, and without any decipherable direction signs.[114] As we shall see, these are to be found absolutely everywhere. There is no limit to the number of imaginable labyrinth patterns.

Einstein's universe, trapped (but also constructed) by the stealth of photons giving a mirage of boundaries, by the interconvertibility of matter and energy, is a labyrinth, a diabolic labyrinth filled with galaxies like so many torqued shells on endless beaches, each stuffed full of their own labyrinths. Heisenberg's atomic matter is also a labyrinth of labyrinths, marked everywhere by dual pathways of uncertainty principles and quantum mechanics. Our nervous system, reporting on such labyrinthine events, is also constructed by labyrinthoid principles, thereby imposing labyrinths upon labyrinths. Chaos theories, fractal geometries, fields regulating morphogenesis, population dynamics of species, myth cycles of tribal peoples are all labyrinths. Labyrinths inevitably seep from domains of nature, where they are ubiquitous, seamless, and fractally nested upon and within one another, to the more modest but also more semieological realms of culture, where they are cruder, more fragmentary, and artificial (meaning also "crafted by artifice"). Artificial labyrinths may not be as daunting or ingenious as those of Nature (or God), but they are human in scale and meaning, thus contain resolutions and even possibilities of accomplishment and victory; they define our peculiar human journey. How can one compare a megalithic cathedral of stones to the universe itself except to point out that the former can take the place of the latter as a replica of human destiny, not to speak of the fact that of course humans can create a Stonehenge, a Chartres, a Serpent Mound, but not a galaxy.

A labyrinth is an opaque place of paths whose routes need obey no prior law. It may be ruled by chance or improbability, signaling the defeat of pure Reason.

A labyrinth always has a dual character, since path may be substituted for wall. The path leads to one goal, and the wall to another. The pattern may be simple—a spiral or a twisted road that nevertheless has no dead ends. In this type one cannot lose one's way; the technical term for it is "unicursal." On the other hand, it may be complex, with dead ends and recursive loops; in this type one may become lost, and it is known as "multicursal."[114] But I shall refrain from further use of such needlessly complicated terminology.

Finally, a labyrinth is itself enclosed within a border: a square, circle, or any other figure.

The complexity of a labyrinth is measured by the minimum number of choices necessary in order to arrive at the goal. A labyrinth with one or more centers is generally more complex than a labyrinth with an exit.[106]

One must also distinguish between extricable labyrinths, which must yield eventually to patient exploration of all possible paths, and inextricable labyrinths, where one can become lost in an endless array of loops and dead ends. Certain inextricable labyrinths with a center that cannot be reached are called impenetrable.

There is also a distinction made between the maze, where several paths lead to the same goal, and the labyrinth, which has a unique path leading to an exit or center. In a maze, there is one path that is shorter than others, but this does not apply to a labyrinth.

We must also note the difference between the representation of a labyrinth, as seen from above in a kind of schematic view, and its reality as experienced from inside, where it may appear to be a succession of dark caves. Those who actually walk through labyrinths—"maze treaders," as they are known in England—have a confused view of what the road must be but are unaware of its complexity, which they only discover as they advance little by little. The "maze viewers" who look upon it from above can immediately discern its complexity but do not undergo the same experience of ignorance and straying. The labyrinth is constructed primarily to be walked, without being known or represented to the walker.

This Book Is a Labyrinth

I shall begin with an account of the history of labyrinths, whose incredibly universal presence strikes us with a poignant and universal meaning. Then I shall explain how they can help us comprehend the future in all its dimensions: economic, political, scientific, esthetic, and philosophical, and then how they allow us to act upon this future. Finally, I shall discuss what one may hope to gain from such initiatory voyages, and how to learn labyrinthine thinking.

By the end of this book, I hope the reader will know better how to tread the paths of the future. But first, we must retraverse the long and meandering history of humanity, drawing upon its wisdom that comes to us from afar. Hence this book cannot proceed in a straight line. Like any initiatory quest, it is arranged like a labyrinth, and one must accept the possibility of getting lost and having to backtrack as we advance unremittingly towards an invisible center, eyes and ears keenly attuned to the counsels and signs to be encountered at the turning of certain pages.

Perhaps doing this will help us better understand that time itself does not flow but is spread out in space with comings and goings, with spirals and blind alleys, and distant proximities as well as illusory distances. Perhaps we will retain a recognition that the Wisdom of the future, the one that will save humanity from suicide, is one that has nothing to do with saving time, but with filling it, living it so as to take its full measure. Perhaps we will see that nothing is more urgent than the learning of patience and the pleasure of losing oneself, of ruses and detours, dances and games, so as to discover oneself as capable of fashioning one's life as an ironic work of art—before one is able, if ever, to pass on its secret.

The *Labyrinth* in *Culture* and *Society*

Approach

This section provides a succinct history of labyrinths, from their first appearances to their demise and current resurrection.

Birth

First Spirals, First Labyrinths

The idea of the spiral surely arose from observation of such things as seashells, whirlpools, whirlwinds, and typhoons—it is a natural maritime pattern.

The idea of the labyrinth surely arose from explorations of caverns and grottos, from traversing forests, and from contemplating the course of rivers, with their meanderings and their network of tributaries (see illustration #55). It is a natural terrestrial pattern.

The spiral is smooth, regular, ordered, and of heavenly inspiration. The labyrinth is tortuous, convoluted, disordered, and of human inspiration. It is surely not unrelated to a sense of the first path a human being ever travels, at the end of which he or she becomes a person: the path that leads out of the maternal womb. *Every human being's first labyrinth is that of woman.*

It is astonishing that representations of it appear simultaneously in all regions of the planet, ten thousand years before our era. On every continent, we see figures like tiny icons carved on walls, engravings on tombs, paths traced on the ground, interlocking corridors, and ingenious pathways laid in stone.

Stylized meanders have been noted in drawings of birds in the Ukraine, dating from around fifteen thousand years ago. The oldest known graphic representation of a labyrinth was found in a Paleolithic tomb in Siberia: a seven-circuit maze surrounded by four double spirals, carved upon a piece of mammoth ivory. During the same era, the inhabitants of the caves of Altamira and Lascaux must have thought of these places as what we now call labyrinths. The people who came there for refuge drew spirals and meanders as well as animals, leaving mysterious messages from strange ceremonies that became the founding rites of new religions.

Neolithic labyrinths are found in the most diverse locations: on the shores of the Danube and the Aegean, in Iran and the French Savoy, in Ireland, Sardinia, Spain, and Portugal. They were drawn on figurines of the Vinca culture at Brdo, near Belgrade, seven thousand years ago, as well as on feminine representations found at Kirkmedrine, in Scotland.[87] Most of these drawings are inscribed in squares or circles (see illustration #5), but others form bears, birds, and serpents. At Hosur Talup, near Madras in India, the ruins of Kunlani contain numerous stone labyrinths that resemble the pebble circles dating from the same period in Scandinavia.[87] Analogous designs are still found in the Hogar, in the Jebel Bes Seba, and in the Sahara among the Yombas of Mauritania, one of whose creations is a giraffe contemplating a labyrinth, in which there is a bird fascinated by a serpent.[114]

Drawings of this era were no longer limited to isolated designs on walls or ground but were often a series of well-appointed caves whose walls were decorated with labyrinthine drawings. At New Grange, there is a sort of pattern carved upon the stones of a cave, with one particular flagstone at the entrance engraved with a triple spiral (see illustration #8). At the opening to a cavern near Boisney in Cornwall, one finds two labyrinths engraved on a stone table. Another is found on a block of granite, carved over six thousand years ago in the caves of the Wicklow Mountains in Ireland.[114] On the island of Gavrinis facing the Breton town of Vannes, a mysterious serpentine gallery was organized for habitation five thousand years ago—its main corridor divides into three branches, and every change in direction is indicated by crosses, spirals, and cross-hatchings—a cultural puzzle that has yet to be solved (see illustration #9).[20] Another labyrinthine cavern set up nearly four thousand years ago at Val Cormonica in Italy is covered with flamboyant spirals (see illustration #7).

The Seventh Wonder of Egypt

The oldest known Egyptian labyrinthine drawing was found at Memphis on a fragment of a soapstone pail. Two human silhouettes face each other next to a sort of spiral made up of five turns around a center. At the same time and place, the first explicitly labyrinthine funerary monuments appear.[33] Entirely artificial in construction, they are designed to confuse anyone who does not know their pattern. These reveal one of the primary functions of the labyrinth, which is akin to that of the pyramids: preventing access by strangers to tombs of royalty, and keeping the secret of this voyage so that none can come to make off with the objects therein. Undoubtedly there existed previous labyrinths elsewhere that served such a function, but these are the first to be clearly identified as such. The oldest of these labyrinth-tombs was built some fifty-five centuries ago, during the same period when the stone circles of Stonehenge were being erected. It harbored the remains of Peraben, a second-dynasty pharaoh.[113] Apparently this was a relatively uncomplicated structure, and subsequent monuments multiplied in both number and complexity, becoming substitutes or annexes to pyramids. Fifteen centuries later, the tomb of Amenemhet III, built near a town now called Medinat al-Fayum, manifested an unbelievable complexity (see illustration #12). Constructed to glorify the union of twelve provinces to form a single empire, it brought together the tombs of the twelve princes who had agreed to combine their domains and mortuaries. It was established near the lake of Moeris, a containment pool for the Nile near the pyramid of Hawara. Also dedicated to the glory of Sobek, the sacred crocodile, it made such an impression on all who approached it that the Greeks classed it as one of the Seven Wonders of the world.[113] Although it is now destroyed, the accounts of Greek and

Roman historians and geographers have given us numerous descriptions of the parts of it that were open to visitors. Thus Herodotus, who composed the oldest known treatise on the labyrinth, described its first, and only accessible level, as "the labyrinth of Egypt" some twenty-five centuries ago; it had been built fifteen centuries before his time. His account gives an idea of the giddiness that must have overtaken visitors who passed through these twelve connecting covered courtyards, sitting upon a double series of 1,500 rooms built on two levels: "The rooms we walked through, the courtyards in which we wandered, spoke to us in their astonishing variety. We marveled endlessly as we moved from a courtyard to an apartment, from this apartment into porticos, and from these porticos into new courtyards. The roof is built entirely of stones, like the walls, and the walls are covered with sculpted figures. Each of the courtyards is surrounded by a colonnade made of white, perfectly placed stones. At the corner where the labyrinth ends, there is a pyramid measuring forty orgyies in height."[66] The passageways that lead from room to room are described as "very interlinked," and they "cause a perpetual swoon." On the lower floor were the tombs of the twelve princes and the sacred crocodiles. "If one were to bring together all the walls and buildings built by Greeks, the totality would still appear as smaller, both in the labor and the expense it represents, than this labyrinth...even greater than the Pyramids."[66] Four centuries later, the Roman Pomponius Mela gave another, equally panegyric description in which he named the architect: "This work of Psammétion contains three thousand apartments and twelve palaces in a single walled enclosure. It is covered with marble. There is only one passage downward, but once below, there is an infinity of routes through which one passes and re-passes, with a thousand detours, thus plunging one into uncertainty, because one often returns to the same places after turning around and around. One finds oneself back at the same point of departure, yet one knows not how to get out."[114] Later, during the reign of Augustus, Diodorus of Sicily wrote of it with the same sense of bewilderment. Shortly afterward, Pliny describes this same edifice, built 1,600 years before his time, as "one of the most extraordinary works to which human beings have ever devoted their efforts."[114] Just after the beginning of our era, Strabo marveled, in his *Geographia,* at its "covered passageways with intermingling corridors, linked together in such a way that no stranger could succeed in finding his way, either out of it or into it, without a guide."[114]

Ultimately it was plundered by the Romans as a stone quarry, and nothing remains of it today.

The Cretan Maze

After its beguilement of the Egyptians, the labyrinth took hold in the Cretan civilization next door. It occurs not only in the creation of fables, as in that most beautiful of myths, the story of Theseus, but also in actual design and construction. For Cretan labyrinths are not limited to stories about Minos. Although no absolutely certain remains of such a monumental labyrinth have been found, there have been many discoveries of caves that have been built up so as to function as labyrinths. There are also many vases and medallions on which the Theseus myth is represented (see illustrations #17 and #21). At the beginning of the second millennium before our era, when Knossos and scores of other Cretan cities became a flourishing civilization, the "first awakening, the first smile, the first gestures of young Europe," the labyrinth is already omnipresent.[47] The primary of all these in the collective imagination is of course the one where Minos is supposed to have enclosed the Minotaur, and which was long confused with the palace of Knossos (see illustration #22).

In fact, Cretan civilization, though one of the most powerful in the ancient Mediterranean world, has not left a quantity of unambiguous ruins. It is at least certain that the city Knossos existed, and that it was the thriving capital of a splendid civilization forty centuries ago, before being sacked around 1400 B.C. by Achaean Greeks, immediately after an earthquake and an explosion of the volcano Thera. According to Homer, it was "the great city of that King Minos, whom the great Zeus took as his confidant every nine years." The end of the Trojan war three centuries later coincides with that of Knossos.[46]

Minos may well have been one of its rulers, but his personality remains elusive. In some tales he appears as a great king, wise and discerning. By contrast, the eleventh book of the *Odyssey* describes him as having a "malevolent mind." Euripedes paints him as a debauched tyrant who ravages the Peloponnesus and the Cyclades. The dates of his reign are uncertain as well: according to Herodotus, a contemporary of Sophocles, he lived three generations before the capture of Troy, around 1260 B.C., but Homer places him a generation before this.[46] A marble inscription found at Paros mentions a King Minos, founder of Kydonia in Crete, which could date him in 1445, 1433, 1319, or 1285 B.C. Eusebius claims that he lived in the fourteenth century B.C.[14] But other authors, such as Plutarch and Diodorus of Sicily, make a distinction between two kings named Minos: one was the son of Zeus and the other was his grandson. For still other chroniclers, "Minos" serves as the name of a dynasty of the second millennium before our era.[141]

Several modern theorists see this legend as a simple myth without any historical foundation in an identifiable monarch: a Solar figure whose powers are renewed every nine years by human sacrifice and by the remarriage of the King in the disguise of a bull (representing the Sun) with the Queen in the disguise of a cow (representing the Moon).[114] Others say that every Cretan ruler, in the costume of a son of Zeus, had to consult the god every nine years—every hundredth month—at the center of the island. If Zeus was displeased with him, he did away with him; otherwise, he revealed to him the laws that must be obeyed for the next hundred months.[46] Hence the sacrifice of the Minotaur would be simply the foundation story for the enthronement rite of every Cretan king.

The Minotaur himself is just as elusive as his father. For some, he is merely the offspring of the adulterous liaison between Queen Pasiphaë and Taurus, a general who served under a king named Minos. For others, he might even be the reincarnation of Talos, murdered by his uncle Daedalus.

Talos, often known as Perdix, is himself an especially enigmatic figure in this story, where he makes only a brief appearance. Some credit this "able man of skillful hands" (the meaning of his surname) with the invention of the compass, others with that of the fishhook, the raft, bricks, or magical bows.[56] Some see him as no more than a man of cunning. Still others make him into a frightening survivor of the race of bronze, creatures made by Hephaistos in Sardinia, using the process of lost wax casting. They had a single vein, closed at their heel by a bronze pin. This race was appointed by Zeus to be guardians of Crete, and they exterminated invaders by hugging them to their own bodies, which had been heated to a red-hot glow.[56]

The existence of the Labyrinth of Knossos is also far from certain. For some, including the archeologist Sir Arthur Evans, the king's palace, known as the palace "of the double axe," is itself the very Labyrinth whose center held the Minotaur prisoner (see illustration #22). This ritual enclosure, named the *Deidaleion,* is mentioned in Linear B tablets found in the ruins of the palace of Knossos. Other writers, Sophocles among them, depict the Labyrinth as a cavern. Still others claim it was a prison built inside the city; Plutarch describes it as such in his life of Theseus: "According to the Cretans…the Labyrinth was a prison whose only terror was the impossibility of escaping, once one was shut inside it." Some geographers of the second-century B.C. locate it at Gortyne, others at Knossos.[141] Even more simply, for some scholars the Labyrinth is merely the bed set up by Daedalus as the love nest of Pasiphaë and General Taurus.

It also appears that the reality of the legend of the Labyrinth might correspond to a series of underground galleries that can be explored today, located two kilometers northwest of Skotino, a four-hour walk to the east of Knossos.[141] It contains many galleries, converted and arranged on four levels, with bearded feminine faces and limestone sculptures depicting quadrupeds (see illustration #18).

The same confusion reigns when it comes to other subjects of the myth—for example, the function of Ariadne's thread. Pherecydes, who saw it only as a mnemonic device for finding the path of return, wrote: "Ariadne gave Theseus a spool of thread that she had received from Daedalus, and instructed him to tie its end to the door of entry, unwinding it as he advanced, until he came upon the most secret chamber...and then to return again by rewinding the thread."[114] Others maintained that it was the magic thread itself that guided Theseus towards the center of the Labyrinth. Still others say that it was in fact a heavenly spiral, or else a luminous crown, both talisman and beacon (see illustration #21). And there are many even today who still wonder why Ariadne did not accompany Theseus into the interior of the cavern....

The story of Icarus has its own variants (see illustration #25b). Some maintain that Daedalus and his son in fact fled Crete by ship, and that Daedalus had actually invented the sail, rather than artificial wings, to escape the pursuing galleys of Minos. In these versions, Icarus died rather stupidly, simply toppling from the railing.

"Labyrinth" also referred to caves of youthful initiation rites, to palace architecture, and to cities. Later, designs of labyrinths appeared on coins, always with the same seven-circuit pattern that was found previously in Egypt and carved in the granite of the Wicklow Mountains.[113] These designs, which the Greeks called "shell-formed places," like the myths that are associated with them, seem to be inspired by Egyptian funerary monuments. This is plausible, because there were abundant exchanges then between Egyptian civilization, which was at its apogee, and the thriving young Cretan civilization. The same design reappears a thousand years later at Pylos, and at the entrance to the temple of Asclepios, at Epidauros in Greece. Seven centuries later we find it in the Alps, and then at Pompeii during the first century A.D. (see illustration #29).[14]

Tombs and Mandalas

Elsewhere during the same era, the labyrinth is found among a very large number of peoples. There are stone designs in Babylon (see illustration #14), as well as among the Peruvian Nazcas on a plateau of white gypsum covered with a natural manganese varnish; on it is displayed a three-circuit labyrinth twenty meters in diameter, along with animal drawings—eagle, bear, lizard, shark, spider—which themselves form labyrinths (see illustration #67).[93] Both square and circular labyrinths exactly like the Cretan drawings are found engraved on mesa stones among the Hopis, the oldest sedentary tribe in North America, a member of the Anasazi group. In Ohio, on a large earthen structure seven meters wide and four hundred meters long, one discovers the labyrinthine Hopi signature of the serpent, protector of the tribe all through their long voyage to its conclusion in the mountains of the West.[129]

Also during this era in China, labyrinths were carved in the T'ong T'ing ("hollow mountain") grotto. These were also used to form incense trails, the slow burning of which serves to measure the passage of time. Sometimes they are of exquisite refinement, with different perfumes used for different hours. In general, these incense labyrinths are used at night, when the time cannot be told from the sun. They were supposedly invented during a time of great drought, when water clocks could not be used. Incense labyrinths are mentioned in a poem by Yan Jiangpu some 2,500 years ago.[124] Later developments of this became copper vessels with extremely complex grooves where each one of the hundred forks indicates one *kal,* a division of the day. But as few as five divisions might be used, and there were different labyrinth lengths according to the season (see illustration #61). [124]

Tibetans designed a special form of labyrinth in some of their mandalas—complex images composed of circles and squares with pathways and dead ends. Labyrinths can still be seen today in the caves of India and in the Roman catacombs at Postumia, near Trieste. The foundations of the Acropolis, as well as those of the tomb of Augustus Caesar at Rome, follow a labyrinthine pattern.

So far, we have found no evidence that any of these stone, vase, and wall engravings were necessarily building plans for monuments. The first drawing that is thought to be certain as a graphic scheme for labyrinthine architecture is that of the Cretan palace built at Pompeii a century before our era. Its form is that of a mosaic graffito on the wall of the house of Marcus Lucretius (see illustration #26). During the same period, Pliny reported having seen four labyrinthine monuments, "the most astonishing work of mankind, and there is nothing fictional whatsoever about it."[114] One of them was in Egypt, another in Crete, the third in Lesbos, and the fourth in Italy, constructed by Porsenna, king of Etruria, which was surmounted by pyramids 150 meters high. He also said that Romans planted grass labyrinths as a children's amusement—this is the first mention of labyrinth plantations, which would become so popular 1,500 years later.

Labyrinth figures are also found on Roman seals and tombs. They were seen also at entrances to Celtic fortresses in Ireland, Gaul, and Brittany, as at Meiden Castle in Dorset, and on a great number of other sites of this type.[14] In Scandinavia, figures are often composed of stones placed on sand (see illustration #10) along the coast and at the entry to the harbors of Lindbacke, Nyköping, Galgberget, Visby, and Arundehög.[26]

There is one striking omission regarding this universality: there is no mention of a labyrinth as such anywhere in the Bible, even in those passages relating events that were contemporary with Cretan civilization. But the protective walls of Jericho could be considered to represent an indirect reference (see illustration #33).

The Christian World

When Christianity came along, instead of wiping out or combating the symbols of previous cults, the new religion absorbed and appropriated them. Deities became saints, temples became cathedrals, amulets were venerated as relics, and pastoral festivals were celebrated as events in the life of Christ. Labyrinths found a natural role in tombs and in cruciform sacred spaces. The oldest known labyrinth traced on the floor of a church dates from 328. It was found in the basilica of Reparatus, in the Algerian town formerly known as Orléansville (see illustration #31).[113] In its center are the two words "SANCTA ECLESIA," repeated in every possible direction of reading, forming a square of thirteen letters. The second surviving labyrinth of this type was drawn two hundred years later on the floor of the church of Saint Vidal of Ravenna.

Subsequently, labyrinths were inscribed on floors in virtually every church and abbey of Christendom. Generally they were engraved after completion of the nave of the church. One finds such majestic and mysterious designs in church entrances at Chartres, Sens, Amiens, Reims, Saint-Quentin, Bayeux, Arras, Poitiers, and in the abbeys of Saint-Martin at Saint-Omer (see illustration #41), of Santa Maria Trastevere at Rome, San Michele Maggiore at Pavia, and others at Cremona, Lucca, and Saint Mary of Agnesi at Plaisance.[118] Most of them contain eleven circuits (twelve if the center is included) and are circular in shape, as at Chartres, although some are octagonal, as at Amiens, and more rarely square, as in the ancient North African basilica.[114] Almost all consist of a unique, nonforking path leading only to the center, with the exceptions of those at Ravenna, Poitiers, and Saint Omer (see illustrations #37, #41, and #42). In Gothic cathedrals such as the one at Chartres, the labyrinth is placed on the axis of the nave (see illustration #38), which itself is oriented towards the point of sunrise on the Saint's day associated with the monument. If the cathedral's design is seen as a representation of Christ on the cross, the labyrinth is at the level of the thighs, governed by Sagittarius, which is also the sign of travel and pilgrimage.[133]

In the earliest basilicas, one often finds a Minotaur figure, with man's head and bull's body, at the center of the labyrinth. Later, this is replaced by a cow with a human head, for example in the church at Saint Omer. Still later edifices have a figure of

Jesus at the center. In the center of the labyrinth at Saint Gall, one can read the words *"Domus Daedali";* in the one at Saint Michael of Pavia, the inscription states that "Theseus entered and killed the monster."[106] Along the length of the labyrinth of the dome at Lucca are written three verses that refer back to Theseus. In Notre Dame of Amiens, as in many other churches, the central stone of the labyrinth bears a copper plaque marked with the emblem of the architect-builders of the cathedral.[133] Writings of the period refer both to labyrinths and to master architect-builders as *daedali;* the labyrinth thus had become a kind of signature of masons such as Robert de Luzarches and Thomas de Cormont at Amiens, Jean d'Orbais at Reims, and the mysterious Écarlate of Chartres.

Other names besides *daedalus,* were "Saint Jacques Road," "Jerusalem Road," "Solomon's Prison," or French words such as *méandre, or lieue* (=league), because it was said that the same time was required to traverse the labyrinth on ones knees as to walk a league normally (see illustration #44). In fact, it took a good hour to kneel one's way through the *lieue* of the cathedral of Sens, which was destroyed in 1768. The so-called *lieue de Jérusalem,* in the thirteenth-century collegiate church of Saint-Quentin, was described in a chronicle of that time as being "composed partly of black and partly of white tiles, with circles and detours constructed with such industry and proportion that often attracted the curiosity of visitors, if they were allowed to walk in this church. It is octagonal, and thirty-five feet in diameter, with a stone of the same shape in the center...."[133]

Just as we see the presence of the labyrinth everywhere in medieval places of worship, so we find it, along with other engraved symbols, in the Masonic signatures in castle stones as well: in the spandrel of the castle of Moissac, on the spiral stairway of Saint-Gilles, and at Vézelay on the famous bas-relief celebrating the change from the old to the new Covenant, it is engraved on the garments of both Jesus and Moses (see illustration #80). It is present in alchemy and even in music with the advent of polyphony, especially in the form of the fugue, a veritable labyrinth in sound.

Even today, our sedentary civilization can be thought of as a labyrinth of labyrinths. We still have need of the labyrinth, in order to explain and understand ourselves.

Living

Now I shall make an attempt to decode the meaning of all these figures.

Every Drawing Has a Meaning

How are we to explain the universal presence of this figure in all civilizations? Is there an explanation common to all these cultures, or must we consider each case separately? Is the labyrinth a random sort of graffito, a gratuitous riddle, a work of art, a game, a prison, a stronghold, a place of prayer, a tool of initiation—or is it a coded message?

It is my contention that the labyrinth is the material manifestation of a collective unconscious, of a message sent forth into the beyond. It represents the first abstraction of a sense of human destiny, of an ordering of the world. It describes the universe in both its visible and invisible aspects—a universe whose traversal, like that of life, is both sought after (because it leads to the discovery of eternity) and feared (because nothingness waits there). It is like a place of precarious and dangerous passage, a breach between two worlds.

In all civilizations, the labyrinth serves first as symbol, then as basis of myth, and finally as mode of subliminal communication. Thus it shows itself to be something like a sophisticated mode of expression, *a language before writing.*

Labyrinths are the only meaningful kind of graffiti that occur among the earliest peoples; before writing, even before picture-poems, every drawing expressed a concept, and every figure was

retreated, turned, circled back on their steps, became lost, and despaired. In the Pacific Ocean (which of course was differently named among different peoples), nomads traveled by canoe among strange new islands, losing stars along the horizon behind them while new stars arose out of the sea ahead of them, from Asia through Micronesia and Polynesia to New Zealand and Australia. Their characters were forged in the course of these long voyages, where the aim was survival.

Thus every human being still shares these feelings of going astray, becoming hopelessly lost, regretting one's entry into this life, having been forced into it—expelled into this labyrinth of existence, from that other protective labyrinth of the womb. Having been born, one still ventures forth, defenseless and clueless, full of fear and hope, into the desert, the ocean, the forest, into places of ambush, enemies, and hidden reefs. Compelled to keep going in order to survive, we have wandered and gone astray, at the mercy of storms, avalanches, chasms, glaciers, ferocious beasts, and hostile tribes. Living in constant dread of seeing the road close in front of us, of becoming fatally lost, we simultaneously sense ourselves very close to the goal.

The first of all trials is that of the human being exiled from primordial perfection, as told in all stories of the creation—in the Bible's expulsion of Adam and Eve from the garden of Eden and in the Hopis' story of being chased from the protective underground by Sotuknang and compelled to pass through long, frightening labyrinths through nine successive universes that Taoiwa had prepared for them: "All the lines and passages in the labyrinth form the universal design of the Creator, which human beings must follow in the paths of their own lives."[129]

In their endless treks through labyrinthine deserts, nomads discovered that God was to be found wherever he or she was to be found, and that this was not the God of only one territory. God belongs to humanity, not to the land. This idea of an interiorized God, carried in oneself, always there wherever one goes, necessarily led to the startling discovery of monotheism. Such a departure from pantheism could only occur to a nomad.

It was nomads who were the first to undergo the living ordeal of the House of the Dead. They were the first to risk their lives in deserts in quest of rebirth. And it was they who felt the reality of the labyrinth deeply, for their very lives took the form of mazes, as shown in all their tales of voyages full of meanders.

But with experience, human beings gradually learned to domesticate space. Having found shelter from storms in caverns, they learned to leave the caverns, to cultivate and clear the land, and finally to build houses, palaces, and cities, themselves protected by walls. In order to preserve the memory of the past, they ritualized their passage from the nomadic to the sedentary state: the descent into the shadows of the caves which protected their nomadic ancestors gradually became myth, and the hunting trip a sacred narrative. They invented stories and simulations of pathways and passages, and these simulations took the form of drawings.

At this point, we discern four meanings of the labyrinth, which occur in succession. In the earliest cultures, whether nomadic or sedentary, death is seen as a voyage, and the labyrinth tells primarily of the passage into the beyond, the funeral ritual. As the best graphic symbol of this path, the labyrinth represents a map of the beyond."[78] Once passed away, the deceased are enclosed therein, both for the peace of their own souls, and so they do not return to haunt the living. "It is the path of the House of the Dead."[40] It is the image of twilight, "the spiral castle where the divine Sun-King withdraws after his death, and whence he sometimes returns," the voyage of the dead towards the Earth-Mother.[61] It is during this voyage that the survival and rebirth of the spirit in eternity is decided, according to an exact and solemn conformance to ritual. Just as the deceased must overcome obstacles placed in their paths by gods and other spirits, the living also must protect against their return by placing a labyrinth at entrances to houses or other locations.

This leads naturally to the second meaning of the labyrinth: an account of a trial undergone by an individual or a group. The specific meaning may include a simulation, mime, or dramatization of a ritual of sacrifice, the execution of a scapegoat, or the representation of a primordial regicide, facilitating both the resurrection of the king and the initiation of those participating in the rite.

Now the logic of a third meaning begins to establish itself: any sort of trial, sacrifice, victory over a monster, or winning of treasure, must amount to an initiation, "conscious or unconscious, and therefore an expression of the human condition."[41] Whoever traverses the labyrinth thus becomes an initiate, entering into a new life. In fact, many civilizations have used caverns themselves as places of initiation: youth enter there anonymously, and emerge as adults endowed with names, reborn and full-fledged members of the collectivity.

Now the fourth meaning appears, which is also a development of the first: that of resurrection. To enter the labyrinth, to risk death, to undergo trial and initiation, is to become a hero or heroine. By extension, this becomes the designation of an entirely new person, returned from the land of the dead, perhaps even reincarnated.[40] Thus the labyrinth also becomes a natural representation of a story of healing, of a road of access to eternity. It signifies a resurrection, or at least a profound transformation, of the victor. It also constitutes a border, a place of passage, meeting, and communication between the world of the living and that of the dead. This makes it a very dangerous place.

On the whole, *all labyrinth myths tell, in one fashion or another, this fourfold story: a voyage, a trial, an initiation, and a resurrection.* All of them recount the promise of the hero's death, with its sacrifice, discovery of the initiatory secret, and transfiguration.

This is why labyrinths help us understand the manner in which a given civilization deciphers the secrets of life, death, the beyond, the creation of the world, and the identity of the human being.

First Paradises, First Hells

When tribes became sedentary, first in caverns discovered

along their way, then in huts they built with their own hands, their members would naturally sketch labyrinths as memories of their voyages of old. Caves and grottos were also seen as the gates of entry into the subterranean world where their ancestors came from, and where they would go after death. In fact, all the earliest Creation tales are stories of nomads emerging from underground or perhaps some other place entirely, bearing their sins with them, in order to settle down as sedentary dwellers on this Earth.

A study of the few surviving rites of peoples of this type invariably reveals the omnipresence of labyrinths, explicit or implicit, as well as the four meanings just described.

On the island of Malekula in the New Hebrides, an especially interesting myth is told, in which the labyrinth plays a major role. It is said that after death, every inhabitant of the island departs for Wies, in the land of Serving. Near a rock named Lenbutt Song, at the threshold of the cavern where the dead reside, they meet a feminine spirit named Temes Savsap. Before admitting the new arrival, this guardian spirit draws a labyrinth on the sand, which is called *nahal,* meaning "the road." The guardian allows the deceased to look at it briefly, and then erases half of it. The deceased must restore the drawing exactly, with one movement of the finger, never lifting it from the sand, and then find the path which leads to the center. [30] If the person has been properly initiated in life, studying the sacred designs, the chants, dances and ritual poems, he or she will be able to restore the drawing easily from memory and "traverse" it.[114] But in case of failure, either to make the proper drawing or find the way to the center, the guardian spirit will devour the soul, making it disappear into the void. Hence for the inhabitants of Malekula, a lifelong, intimate knowledge of the rites of the labyrinth and its secrets is necessary for the eternity of their souls.

Another story from the Pacific, this time from the Ceram archipelago of the Spice Islands, sheds a different light on this idea. At the beginning of time, when people were still immortal, a girl was kidnapped by a violent person called "Man of the Sun," who buried her alive until she died. As punishment for this first murder, men became mortal. Later, to redress the balance, women also became mortal. Since then, a yearly nocturnal ritual reminds humans of this girl and her murder, so that they may not forget that killing was the cause of their mortality. During this ceremony, the male and female dancers must form a spiral of nine cycles and go through a labyrinth. Only those dancers who are able to pass through it will return to Earth as human beings after death; the others will always be beasts or spirits.[114] Here again, the labyrinth symbolizes the sacrifice which channels violence and assures eternal life to those who know how to traverse it.

In many other cultures, the labyrinth is also a road of access to the dwelling-place of the dead. To get there, one must typically descend into the bowels of the Earth, passing through caverns and canyons full of ambushes. Among the Bambaras, the spiral symbolizes fecundity, the original Word, the spirit that created the world. For Amerindian cultures of Central America extending to the Mayans, the voyage of death is a long march through an underground labyrinth. In present-day Burma, the family of a deceased person must traverse a labyrinth of bamboo, thus helping the dead person traverse the one on the other side, to arrive at the place of eternal repose. *The Egyptian Book of the Dead* also prepares people for such a voyage of no return, a passage through caverns and blind alleys that are the dens of devouring monsters, at the end of which the ultimate kingdom is found.

The Secret of the Cretans

Cretan labyrinths also depicted the voyage of the departed, even as they served as initiation sites for youth. The entire myth of Theseus is an account of a voyage towards death, sacrifice, rebirth, and initiation. Daedalus is the initiator, the Minotaur is the monster, Ariadne the soul-reward, and Theseus the initiate— much later he is even allowed to descend into Hades and return safe and sound. Physical labyrinths were also clearly places of initiation: in order to attain the status of adults, young Cretans had to climb to the summit of sacred mountains and descend from there by way of canyons and caverns.[141] As preparation for this ordeal, they were grouped into fellowships and trained to hunt without arms, to employ decoys and ruses, to overcome fears of darkness and disorientation, and to fight with adults disguised as monsters. During the voyage of initiation, their families considered them as dead. Having triumphantly emerged from the caverns, they received their arms and civil rights.[46] In Sparta, adolescents also underwent trials before receiving the arms of warriors. They had to get successfully through an ambush of giants, overcome a bull from Crete, and thread their way through a labyrinth. Even today, an analogous ceremony takes place every July 26 at Skotino, near Knossos in Crete. Young people there throw off their children's clothes and dance in honor of Parasceva, also known as Veneranda, a virgin saint of the third century who gained victory over a dragon.[141] One also finds similar themes in pagan Scandinavian legends of the same era.

Eternities by the Thousands

The link between the labyrinth and the journey of the dead is also found in Babylon. At the same epoch as in Crete, the fiend Humbaba, guardian of the land of the dead and enemy of Gilgamesh, is represented with a hideous labyrinthine countenance, composed of viscera and jawbones (see illustration #68). In order to free a damsel held prisoner by Humbaba, Gilgamesh ventured into the monster's domain, a magic forest replete with "secret stairs" and "dead end roads."[14] He freed the girl, killed Humbaba, and became a god. The parallel with the myth of Theseus is obvious, with the forest acting as labyrinth in this case.

All over the world, we also find labyrinths drawn in front of houses, the purpose of which is to trap the spirits of the dead. In China, where the custom is widespread, a spiral is also engraved or painted on funeral urns, to help the departed in their voyage beyond. In Tibet, where resurrection is considered to be the worst thing that can befall the deceased, the *Book of the Dead* explains how the departed face the threat of being drawn back into the cycle of birth, death and resurrection, endless interlocking labyrinths of lives of suffering and dying. The domains of the living and the dead as well as all intermediate and transcendent realms are linked in a series of *bardos* (including this world), a labyrinth out of which one can pass only by recognizing the true nature of existence and incarnation and thereby becoming enlightened. To leave *samsara* and attain *nirvana,* the negation and extinction of the causes of a life of samsaric existence, the sacred book advises the dead person to remain still and seek the ground luminosity behind all consciousness.[123] So that the person praying for the departed may also help all beings to escape and merge into stillness, he or she must contemplate a mandala, concentrating upon its *center,* the symbol of eternal peace.

Certain tattoos among southern Indian people, known as *kulams,* are composed of several rings bound together by a single link; identical to the *nahals* of the island of Malekula, they imprison spirits, trapping them and thereby protecting houses.[30] In the *Mahabharata,* one finds thirteen labyrinth images.[114] These function as mimetic spells, images of traps and dead ends which a good warrior must know how to use to enclose the enemy. In the *Bhagavad-Gita* the labyrinth serves as weapon, fortress, military formation, hypnotic dance, and ruse used by the magician Droma in the battle of Kurushabra in order to confound the enemy. In Australia, aborigines draw *churingas* on blocks of wood or stone.[30] These are combinations of spirals, lines, convolutions, and circles in labyrinthine forms, telling the story of a people, where each symbol designates a person, a deed, or a voyage.[25]

In other civilizations, the labyrinth evokes a different sort of voyage: that of the creation of the universe, or the birth of humanity. Several Amerindian Pueblos tribes, including the Hopis, Zunis, and Pimas, describe their arrival in earthly form as a passage through a labyrinth of underground caverns, following several aborted efforts, due to the people's failure to keep their promises to Taiowa. An echo of these voyages, as well as those of their own nomadic past, is heard in the *Wuwuchim* ceremony of the Hopis, during the ominous period of the shortest day of the year in the dead of winter. The prayer is performed in caverns on their third mesa, facing a circular labyrinth design engraved upon a column set before the sacred altars. This design recalls the Sun-Father, and symbolizes the rebirth of the world after the winter solstice. The Hopis also have a labyrinth which is similar, but of square form, for use in other circumstances, this time related to the Earth-Mother, the cave-dwelling life, and the Kiva, a place of prayer and purification.[129]

In ancient Roman culture, the labyrinth served as image of the Cosmos and the destiny of mankind, and also was related to the voyage of the dead. Virgil tells us that Aeneas was condemned to wander from one maze into another, until he encountered a Cretan labyrinth on the doors of Cumae, at the entrance to Hades, kingdom of the dead.[30] He asked the guardian Sibyl for permission to enter there, in order to see his father Anchises, who had died long ago. She accepted, and he was then able to obtain the Golden Bough which guided him to his father, after which he returned from Hell through the ivory portal, one of the two doors of sleep.[80]

Sinai Is a Labyrinth

We can deduce from the preceding why the Bible excludes the labyrinth from its explicit images: there can be no question of a voyage of the dead in this sense. For the Jews, the dead are not spirits facing eternity, to whom one can address prayers; they are instead abstract elements which belong to an unknowable void, awaiting a collective resurrection. God speaks to living human beings through the medium of his prophets, but no departed soul may speak to the world of the living. This represents the choice of the straight line over the spiral, of transparency over obscurity, the simple over the convoluted, and the unique over the multiple. The People of the Book had need of the arrow which created a sense of History, from the Fall to the Redemption. They refused the cyclic and the reversible. In a sense, they were responsible for the theological straight line, just as the Greeks were for the geometrical straight line.

However, on closer examination, the Bible also speaks of nomads lost in the desert, of threatening spaces, sacred caves, and initiation. And the discovery of God, the learning of his laws and his love, are gained through a succession of trials and sacrifices, initiations and voyages, where the ultimate aspiration is still one of resurrection, collective though it be. If any labyrinth is to be found in the Bible, it would therefore have to represent the collective human voyage from the annihilation of death to the jubilation of the Resurrection. And this labyrinth does exist, a vast labyrinth that is an essential moment in the birth of monotheism, though to my knowledge it has never been identified as such. It is the Sinai, the place of Exodus from Egypt, and in the Old Testament that it plays exactly the same role as the labyrinth does in other cultures. It acts like a maze, blocking the route of the people towards the Promised Land. (Pharaoh said: "The desert has *closed* upon them.") For forty years, an entire generation of the Hebrews wandered there. They even encountered a sort of Minotaur: the Golden Calf, vanquished by Moses/Theseus. But the difference from previous individualistic epics is that it is an entire people who traverse the labyrinth and who are literally reborn in it. None of the adults who first entered the labyrinth left it alive—Moses himself died at the threshold of the Promised Land. This desert-labyrinth gives birth to a chosen people from the country of the dead, initiating them into the messianic life. This is exactly the drama that had to be created in order to do away with individual resurrection, in favor of a collective *parousia*.

Pilgrimages and Processions

In the New Testament, the labyrinth can also be found by reading between the lines. Jesus was born in a grotto-like space, and his body was also laid in a cave; the Calvary is a path of trials and stations which finally ends in resurrection—which has now become individual once more. In the doctrines of a Church that was keen on appropriating previous pagan myths for itself, the labyrinth could not fail to find a prominent place. Very early on, the Christian religion recommended that the faithful seek salvation by following the same path as Jesus, the new Theseus, and to trust in the new Ariadne of the Christian faith. When this alien religion later infiltrated ancient rites, setting labyrinths on sacred temple floors just as they had existed on those of pagan temples, its theologians could easily establish a translation of the ancient maze-legends into a pedagogical story of the Christian faith.

Over the centuries, the pagan treasure was slowly and discreetly absorbed. Sometimes secret messages were inscribed, reflecting struggles between various sects for control of Christianity. Thus in the fourth-century basilica of Reparatus previously mentioned, the *Sancta Ecclesia* is read like a fourfold Greek gammadion, as if referring to the Gnostics for whom Ariadne is the Holy Church.[113]

As in all previous sacred edifices, the labyrinth long served essentially as a kind of magical sign intended to trap evil spirits and prevent them from doing harm. Placed so that the faithful would have to cross it, it later became the more specifically Christian path of salvation, leading to the altar where the ceremony of resurrection was performed. There are very few texts of the period that clearly explain the special ritual role of this design on the floor, as if the secret of labyrinthine initiation should remain the closely guarded privilege of a mystic elite—or as if the Church itself felt some embarrassment at not being able to dispense with this pre-Christian symbol. For example, there is the terse commentary by the twelfth-century Archbishop Boisdefin de Laval, concerning the labyrinth of Embrun: "By means of this labyrinth, it might be understood that the grace of God is addressed to us, so as to find the way, the road to eternal Life."[114] But does this *us* refer to the individual, or does it refer to the Christian faithful as a whole? A felicitous ambiguity…and it so happens that the motto chosen by the Archbishop of Embrun is taken from a statement that Virgil attributes to Jupiter: "Fate will know well enough, how to find its way."

From this century on, the Christian appropriation of the labyrinth becomes even more explicit. At its center, Christ now appears instead of Theseus, the Virgin in place of Ariadne, and sin in the place of the Minotaur. This translation of the myth is even overtly advocated—in a manuscript of this period discovered at Munich, we find Theseus presented as a kind of pre-figuration of the Christ because, like the latter, he "destroyed death and liberated life" (see illustrations #30 and #32).[114] By the fourteenth century, Theseus has been universally and explicitly replaced by Christ, who, by grace of the guiding thread of divinity wound upon the spool of humanity, overcomes the devil rather than the Minotaur. In some cases it is Pasiphaë who is transformed into the Church, tempted now by the devil rather than by Poseidon. Other times, Jesus is Daedalus, ascending to the heavens, while Icarus is replaced by the figure of the devil losing his way.[113] But in any case, the labyrinth is always telling the pilgrim that the Church represents freedom from anguish in the maze of life.

From this point on, the labyrinth is also established as a symbolic image in the lives of individual Christians, threatened by the dead ends of temptation and sin. Langland, in *Piers the Plowman,* describes human destiny as an attractive but morally dangerous labyrinth from which only the Church can help people to escape.[114] One also finds the following epitaph, displayed today in the Museum of Lyon: *"Me caput april ex hoc requit laberinto."* ("April's beginning freed me from this labyrinth.") The labyrinth is also used to explain to the faithful the mystery of the grace of inexplicable decisions: it is just when one feels that one is closest to grace that one is actually farthest; and it is when one feels farthest from it that one is actually closest.[109]

Church labyrinths also served a concrete and practical function that was not only metaphorical: they were the site of a virtual voyage, where the faithful walked in an almost immobile procession towards Jerusalem. This took the form of processions inside places of worship, but also out of doors, especially during times of pilgrimage.

Europe was very much on the move in this sense. Pilgrims were scattered over an entire continent, forming an unimaginably vast labyrinth of complex itineraries with blind alleys, ordeals, and passages leading to a myriad of centers: sanctuaries, reliquaries, and sites of miracles (see illustration #39). Through these meanderings, medieval believers attempted to escape material bonds, to undergo initiation and self-sacrifice, to find eternal life—the same aspirations associated with the labyrinth since the dawn of time. As Goethe observed, these living labyrinths "created Europe" over the course of two centuries. The continent became an inextricably tangled network of routes of nomadicized pilgrims. They lived dangerously, getting lost, dying, meeting with thousands of obstacles worthy of the Minotaur. In the intoxication of being on the road, they also found freedom from bonds of family and social obligations. Grace itself was Ariadne's thread for these medieval pilgrims, walkers in life as in death. The aged and the sick were also among them, marching endlessly across Europe, the mystical desert, so as to play their own part in a redemptive suffering, self-knowledge, and purification through walking towards the light. Like the true nomads of old, they lived in uncertainty: death could come at every turn of the road.[137] Their itinerary was not predetermined, for it consisted simply of a goal to be found at the end of a vague route, filled with halts, more often justified by the need to visit a holy place than by material or logistic reasons. The goals of such pilgrimages were primarily whatever sanctuary of sacred relics happened to be nearby, then Jerusalem and the Holy Sepulcher, and then Saint Jacques (Saint James) of Compostela, especially when the Holy Land became inaccessible. Enormous crowds came to pray at the tomb said to contain relics of Saint James the Elder, sometimes known as *le Matamore,* often considered to be the brother of Jesus, as well as the first martyr after him. He was the patron saint of stonecutters, vagabonds and nomads...and his death had taken place on the Galician coast twelve centuries earlier, at a place which happened to be the site of a five-thousand-year-old petroglyphic labyrinth, identical to those in Crete and the Celtic isles...this labyrinth was symbolized by a shell, which also became the sign of recognition among the pilgrims of Compostela.[7]

But any other sort of nomad, whose wanderings took place outside this ritual, was the enemy: beggar, foreigner, Jew, sometimes also a powerful knight, always mercenary. This sort stole, and brought Evil, sickness or war with him. He was to be driven away, combated, or imprisoned out of charity.[2]

Alchemy and the Kabbalah

During these times the labyrinth also began to be seen as symbolic of the path of wisdom, infiltrating the most secret theological reflections of the other two monotheisms.

This first occurred in Judaism, where the explicitly labyrinthine wisdom of the Kabbalah was systematized as a quest for hidden paths of wisdom, bringing words of very different meanings into relation by comparing their numerological letter values. Correspondences that defied all logic were revealed to connect words with concepts very distant from them; the adept had to pass from one letter to another until he arrived at the first, which was the domain of absolute knowledge. "It shall be thus until man comes to the letter Aleph, the dwelling place of the Master of the world." Still more explicitly, the Kabbalah organizes its teaching around a completely labyrinthine metaphor, the Tree of Life, which connects the ten dimensions of God via twenty-two paths, corresponding to the twenty-two letters of the Hebrew alphabet. The sage must spend his entire life passing through this Tree, this labyrinth, according to a very precise itinerary that begins with the *Keter,* the crown, representing the spirit, and progresses towards the *Malkhout,* the kingdom, which represents matter. In this, he must embark upon a specific succession of paths, called "The Lightning Flash," which traverse, one after another, the ten dimensions of God, and bring about actions of equilibrium, flowering, and retreat, in that order. For the Kabbalist, following this wisdom is the only worthwhile path through life. Thanks to it, the initiate becomes eternal. If the supreme degree of knowledge is attained, one may hope to reincarnate oneself, and may even create life oneself, through manipulation of the twenty-two letters and the ten paths, as taught in an obscure and fascinating book, studied continuously for the last thousand years, the *Sepher Yetsira*. This being which the adept creates is called a Golem, evoking a kind of Minotaur, crouched at the end of a labyrinth of words.

During the same era, one finds the labyrinth in Islam, that other religion born of the desert. In the beauty of its texts, the esthetics of its calligraphic designs, and especially in the mysteries of the alchemists, the labyrinth takes its place as an essential element in the ritual quest for eternity. Said to be the Secret of Solomon, it is the image of the "total effort of the work, of the way to follow." It is a means of progress both towards light and towards the most deeply buried seat of consciousness. This is also a way unto the world of the dead, and for alchemists is comparable to desert crossing of mystics, which itself is almost always represented by a spiral. As a designation of this way, European alchemists used the word "vitriol," initial letters of the Latin phrase: *Visita Interiora Terrae Rectificando Invenis Occultu Lapidem* ("Visit the insides of the Earth: through purification, you will find the hidden stone.")[28]

Here once more, we encounter the essence of the labyrinth, buried deep inside the distant recesses of these different theologies. And then, in the full light of day, Reason arrives to banish this essence.

Dying

Beginning with the Renaissance, the labyrinth begins to be erased. Reason defeats it in the prevailing style of discourse on faith, science triumphs over the ruse, mathematics over practical knowledge, realistic life over eternal Life, transparency over obscurity, and the straight line over the convolution. No longer does one prepare for eternity by traversing the labyrinth of life; one instead seeks to gain time to accumulate the means of enjoyment here and now and pass them on to future generations. The straight line becomes the criterion of truth, transparency establishes itself as a moral law, and both of them reign as esthetic ideals.

Doing Away with Meanders

In the maritime realm, the discovery of the New World, even though it happened as the result of an error, marked the end of the meandering sea-voyage of the wanderer, which began with Ulysses. Now the goal of the sailor became the shortest path, the most economical and rectilinear. This could only be fully realized on the open sea, which was finally made fully possible by inventions such as the sextant and chronometer. On land, of course, the straight groove of the wagon-trail had long ago replaced the winding trails of the hunter.

Trading and maritime peoples tend to hold on to certain nomadic characteristics, including knowledge of the navigation secrets enabling sailors to use a labyrinthine map of the sky as a tool for finding their way at sea—employing the principle of the octant rather than the compass. It helps the user determine the position of Mercury (see illustration #59), estimate the length of the voyage, and to tell time.[87] In early times, Cretan navigators and merchants were known as the only ones who dared sail out of sight of land, because they knew how to find their location at sea.

As for northern maritime peoples of Scotland and Sweden, they had a custom of traversing a labyrinth of stones (see illustration #10) on shore, just before boarding their vessel. Its purpose was to invoke the dangers of the sea by miming the progress of the voyage along the path of a maze. (One such pebble labyrinth, located at Visby, was placed at the foot of a gallows, no doubt to prepare the executed for their last voyage.)

Nomadism remains a kind of prerogative of the strongest of sedentary peoples. For power belongs to those who possess superior means of travel, by land or by sea, whether as warriors or merchants. There are other sorts of nomads—brigands, pirates, vandals or beggars—who become the enemies of sedentary peoples, so that the latter protect and fortify themselves. The pilgrimage itself, that ultimate form of nomadism appropriated by the Church, finally came to be seen as a source of problems: it obstructs commerce and weakens the social order. Luther already began to criticize it as an excuse for abandonment of children, and merchants also complained of its encroachment upon their monopoly of the roads. At this juncture, the only form of nomadism that comes to be tolerated is progressively that of merchandise and money.

Walking Straight

Now philosophy joins in, providing a theoretical basis for this new practice of power. Walking straight becomes the emblem of reason. In an important passage in his *Third Discourse on Method,* Descartes advised travelers who are "lost in any forest" not to "wander around, turning this way and that, nor to stay in one place, but to walk as straight as possible in the same direction, never swerving in the slightest from it for weak reasons.... For by this method, they will at least arrive at an end somewhere, and they will likely be better off there than in the middle of a forest."[35]

The metaphor is lucid: the forest of primitive thinking, as dark as Plato's cave, must, so he says, give way to the transparency of the clearing, which only a straight line can be sure of attaining. From this point on, the reasonable chases away the bent, the complex, the obscure, the troubled, the whirlpool, spiral, flow, all that is ambiguous and redundant. The wise man must now seek or reinvent the straight line, transparency, reason, logic, unity, certainty, and progress. Plato replaces Aristotle. The world must not be accepted as it is, but constructed according to an ideal—at any rate, the ideal as conceived by the elite, not necessarily for the people, who continue to live mostly in a mythic universe.

The straight line also triumphs in most forms of artistic expression, beginning with the Renaissance: in painting and in architecture with the use of perspective, in literature with classical drama and the canons of Malherbe and Boileau, as in music with Haydn and Handel.

From the time of Erasmus, Milton, and Locke, philosophers even begin to use a new pejorative term, "labyrinthine thought," serpentine thinking that winds along, turning back on its path, instead of progressing by a series of logical demonstrations, denounced as "Aristotelian thought." In all European languages, the word "labyrinth" becomes synonymous with complex artificiality, pointless obscurity, torturous systems, and an impenetrable forest. "Clear" becomes a synonym for logical. Yet Paracelsus publishes his *Labyrinth of Physicians,* Comenius his *Labyrinth of the World,* and Baltazar Gracián describes Madrid as "a total labyrinth."[109] In English, the word becomes the equivalent of "baroque"; garden mazes are described, so as to avoid the "amazing" connotation of that word, as *troytoussi* (derived from the city of Troy), and one speaks of *threading* or *treading* them. In French, the maze is now known as the "city of Troy," as it is in Swedish; until the sixteenth century, the expression "house of Daedalus" had still been in use.

The word "labyrinth" first appears in French in 1418 (written *labarinte*), and it designates an inextricable enclosure of cut wood. By the time du Bellay uses the word *labyrinth* in 1553, it means only complexity, complication, entanglement, and confusion. After 1677, it is only employed to designate an insoluble puzzle. Nothing of the profound significance of the labyrinth survived. In the great French *Encyclopédie,* there was only a relatively succinct article devoted to it, which was graced by the following doggerel from Corneille himself, speaking of the great Egyptian labyrinth at Lake Moeris:

> *Thousands of different roads of such artifice*
> *Cut everywhere through this great edifice,*

That whoever attempted to escape the plan,
Found himself back on the paths where he began.

The Labyrinth Becomes Evil

Towards the end of the Middle Ages, theology undertook this same revision. No longer seen as a splendid metaphor of human destiny, the labyrinth is now the accursed place of error, sin, and luxury. It no longer protects, nor leads to freedom, and it becomes the prison of the Good and the lair of Evil.[109] The Church now enjoins the faithful to refuse to enter into the winding and inextricable meanders of paganism, to choose the straight and narrow path which leads to the perfection intended by God. Human nature is denounced as naturally labyrinthine and evil. Hell itself is depicted as a labyrinth: as punishment, sinners risk eternal imprisonment in a maze from which only grace can liberate them.[73]

For some fourteenth-century Christian theologians, such as Pierre Bersuire, Benedictine friend of Petrarch, who had a considerable influence on the Renaissance, the sole means of escaping the labyrinth of the human condition was to despise it, quelling it through the force of faith and spirit.[109] Those followers of Daedalus, who would design and construct such artifacts so as to fly by themselves to the heavens, were bound to fall, victims of their own folly and imprudent excess.

The labyrinth is no longer a figure of destiny, but of the evil, disorder, and disobedience of the unfaithful. In his *Liber sine Nomine,* Petrarch describes the Avignon papacy, which he abhorred, as "the third Babylon and the fifth Labyrinth." Boccaccio also used the labyrinth as a symbol of *luxury and heresy,* and a place of perdition through human love. In his eyes, the evil person is doomed to remain prisoner in his own labyrinth, for, like the Minotaur, his soul is prey to terrifying desires.[109] The good man can escape from it, for in him there is a Theseus who can save him from his own depravity. The *winding* (labyrinthine) ways of sin in each of us are contrasted to the *rectilinear* way of virtue. An eighteenth-century Russian icon also describes life as a thirteen-circuit labyrinth (see illustration #45), of which twelve lead to the deadly sins and to the Hells, and only one avoids them and leads to Paradise.

Erasing Mazes

The Church authorities began to see the advantages of straight lines and transparency in regards to cathedrals. From the fifteenth century on, they began to regret having drawn labyrinths on the floors, which now appeared as unwelcome stigmata of the earliest Christianity and more ancient laws. They had already begun physically to remove labyrinths from the floors of many churches. Those that escaped destruction were relegated to mere pretexts for trivial games at most. As early as 1311, the Council of Vienna forbade dances and games in church labyrinths; apparently this was not so effective, for they had to be prohibited again two centuries later, in a decree of the Parliament of Paris of 1538.[14] Up to the time of the Revolution, the bishop and members of the chapters of Reims and Amiens indulged in an Easter Sunday game of tennis on the labyrinth after Vespers, while the choir sang, alternating with the organ. With end of the great pilgrimages and the growing rarity of processions, the labyrinths were forgotten and simply buried beneath carpets or banks of pews. Sometimes they were systematically destroyed, laboriously removing their stones and replacing them with white marble. In 1768, the chapter-house of Sens ordered the destruction of the cathedral labyrinth. The same period saw the destruction of those at the abbeys of Saint Martin, Saint Omer, Poitiers, Toussaint, Auxerre, and Pont-L'Abbé. At Reims in 1779, the Abbot Jacquemart ordered the destruction of the cathedral labyrinth, because "the noise of children and visitors attempting to follow its winding paths offend the devotions of the faithful."[133] At Arras, the labyrinth was destroyed in 1791, as was that of Amiens in 1825. Today, the only remaining examples are those at Saint-Quentin, Bayeux, and Chartres.[14] In Italy and elsewhere, the same practice was followed, so that most of the stonework mazes disappeared or were forgotten.

Garden Mazes

In this universe of the supposed triumph of reason and logic, the only mazes that survived were those of gardens—domesticated forests. In the collective unconscious, the forest had long taken on the character of a hostile symbol, the lair of Evil, danger, where dwelt dragons and savages, thieves and lepers. It was the refuge of bandits and tramps—in sum, of nomads who threaten sedentary society—and it was a forest which marched on Macbeth's castle, and a forest which terrified Tom Thumb. Then arrives the garden labyrinth, which reassured the powerful by taming and ordering the threat, transforming a hostile Nature into a game to be mastered. One can play at being lost in such a labyrinth, facing no more than the thrill of the simulacrum (see illustrations #47 through #49).

This type of artificial landscaping had already existed among the Celts, and in Roman military camps they often served as training courses and as nocturnal protection. These labyrinths had either trenches, dirt walls, or hedges as borders. In the fifteenth century, people began to use them on castle park grounds, sites of the new social power. Every great lord had to have one, as if his noble power needed to display its own labyrinth in order to be recognized by common mortals. It was as if its enigmatic complexity had become the sign of its owner's sophistication, of the nobleman's power to entrap Evil, thus reassuring his subjects.

The Plantagenet Henry II had a labyrinth constructed at his Woodstock Castle, and it was said that he used it for trysts with his mistress, Rosemond Clifford. Queen Eleanor of Aquitaine had this beautiful woman killed when she discovered the secret passage leading from the labyrinth to her chamber. Charles V of France had a maison de Dédale built in the St. Paul gardens in Paris, and François I set a daedalus in the park of Louise-de-Savoie, as did René d'Anjou in the park of the Baugé manor.[113] Charles V, a kind of nomadic emperor, liked to have labyrinths on the grounds of every castle he stayed in, from Prague to Brussels, from Vienna to Seville. In the second half of the sixteenth century, Cardinal Hippolyte d'Este, son of Lucrezia Borgia, had four of them set up at Tivoli.[14] One of the most complex mazes of the century was the one on his property, which was strewn with statues of dwarfs and monsters symbolizing dangers to the human soul. A six-and-a-half-kilometer maze was laid out in Villa Pisani de Stra. The elector Friederich had a labyrinthine garden constructed according a secret Rosicrucian design. Octave Farnèse, son-in-law of Charles V, chose for his emblem a club like that of Theseus, surrounded by three balls of wax and a thread, with the motto *His Artibus* (By These Means).[91] Countless noblemen wore labyrinths on their doublets, signs of membership in esoteric orders.[113] In 1583 at Anvers, Hans Vredeman de Vries drew a series of labyrinthine gardens that he had seen throughout Europe, published in his book *Historia Viridiarorum Formae*.[114] Mme de Sévigné had one at her house at Les Rochers in Brittany. Buffon conceived one for the Jardin des Plantes in Paris, the architect Gabriel designed one at Choisy-le-Roi, as did the gardener Le Nôtre at Chantilly. In the labyrinth at Versailles (see illustration #49), Mansart installed twenty-nine hydraulic statues, illustrating Aesop's Fables, but Marie-Antoinette had them destroyed in 1774.[99] England had labyrinths at Arley Hall, Somerleyton Hall, and Belton House; one at Swainton was known as "Robin Hood's Run." The Sneinton labyrinth in Nottinghamshire was especially famous, but was destroyed in 1797. The one at Hilton in Huntingdonshire, created in 1666, still exists. The most famous of all is that of Hampton Gardens, constructed in 1690 and described by Jerome K. Jerome in *Three Men in a Boat*.[91]

But garden labyrinths are more fragile than those in churches, and their precariousness is such that even in *A Midsummer Night's Dream,* Shakespeare's Queen Titania already complains of their demise: "And the quaint mazes of the wanton green are undistinguishable for lack of treading." Among the most beautiful labyrinths of neglected gardens are those of Saffron Walden in Essex, and at Sneinton, already mentioned. The thriving bourgeoisie continued the tradition in great European gardens, including the English colonies in America, which can still be admired today at the former British governor's estate at Williamsburg.[91]

Amusement Parks and Social Games

In the nineteenth century, this process of trivialization continued, as labyrinths become simple puzzles and popular pastimes. This occurred first in amusement parks, where they had a huge success, fulfilling a social function not unlike that of animal merry-go-rounds: the domestication and distraction of the masses of displaced peasants who had become suburban workers, by offering them ersatz forests in addition to the simulations of animals in these travelling fairs.

It had already turned up in board games of the snakes-and-ladders type such as *le jeu de l'oie,** already known as a "maze game" as far back as the end of the fifteenth century (see illustration #53), when it even had a square called *"Minesthaurus."*[140] It was also a pretext for lovers' exchanges with the invention of the *"Carte du Tendre"* by the *Précieux* social movement; this was a "tender" lovers' map which featured a labyrinth going from regions with titles like "Sweet Favors," to "Mistrust," to "Neglect," to "Indifference," etc. In the nineteenth century, a labyrinth superimposed on a map of Paris was sold in the streets of the city with the title of *Labyrinthe de Crète,* filled with various mythological references (see illustration #54). According to a contemporary account, another one entitled *Au rendez-vous d'Ariane, porte de Minos* had a great success.[122] It was designed by a certain J.-B. Toselli, an army engineer and ice manufacturer. Another similar one, also drawn upon a map of Paris, and called *Au Trocadéro,* was sold for thirty centimes in 1878 as a souvenir of the International Exposition.

By the end of that century, the labyrinth had vanished except for these amusement parks and social games—it had been reduced to an ironically playful challenge, and entirely erased

---

* Translator's note: *le jeu de l'oie,* though not as popular in England, was know there as "the game of goose."

from the paths of wisdom. Industrial societies, obsessed with speed and the straight line, had lost the ancient sense of fullness, the pleasure of concealment and exposure, the intoxication of initiation, the anguish of the beyond. They now preferred simplicity to complexity, and time saved to time spent. The beyond was no longer an eternity to be prepared for, but an accumulation of material goods to be transmitted to the next generation. In a frantic rush towards ever farther and faster movement, there was no more place for meanders. All things were temporary, and needed to be made quickly and simply. This represented a forgetting of the reality of human life, whose essential desire is to go as slowly as possible from birth to death, hoping to have time to make a limitless number of detours.

Access

The labyrinth is now returning full force into all dimensions of human society, replacing and displacing the straight line. Even in our daily lives, each of us encounters labyrinths with increasing frequency, and what is a dead end for one person is often a goal for another.

In some of them, we are totally guided. For example, when you dial a telephone number, the signal traverses a labyrinth without dead ends, with forks that are all preprogrammed by the figures of the number themselves: country, city, neighborhood, exchange, party. Every terminus of any telephone labyrinth is identified by a number. In dialing systems for portable telephones, bifurcations are correlated with persons rather than places.

In other labyrinths, however, one may become lost. Taking the subway, changing buses, walking from one neighborhood to another, searching for a service on the Internet, looking among the shelves in a large department store, walking through a major train station, airport, amusement park, or museum, registering for a university curriculum, looking for a job...and even, as we shall see, dancing, or playing chess, video games, or soccer.

Learning, playing, dreaming, traveling, working, shopping, dancing, having fun, discovering, caring for one's health—in one way or another, all of these are labyrinthine activities. Even eating and making love are not excluded: we shall see that gastronomy and erotic pursuits can also be voyages of initiation, involving extremely sophisticated labyrinths.

For a time, human beings believed they could transform the world into an artifact composed of straight lines and transparent windows. It was a relatively short-lived illusion. The meander has now reinvaded our daily life, as well as science, economics, politics, urban life, painting, literature, and cinema. And gradually, with the return of the nomad (which will be the hallmark of the next millennium), the labyrinth will reclaim a major place in our universe, cracking through the thin coat of rationality with which we had attempted to cover it.

Those who have forgotten the labyrinth's ancient wisdom, who continue to believe that they can live by the cult of reason and efficiency, run the strongest risk of becoming totally lost. But those who patiently apply themselves to rediscovering its secrets, who know how to follow its initiatory paths and thereby resolve the enigma, will be able to navigate through the forests of the future.

Discovering

The Ancients Knew

The ancients knew that the process of discovery resembles moving through a labyrinth, with a constant alternation of proximity and distance to an inaccessible reality. They used the maze as a symbol to represent and think about the universe. But it was especially used to represent phenomena of both nature and thought which, several millennia ago, had already stimulated the concept of the labyrinth as a marker and guide.

Early science, as founded by Archimedes and Lucretius, thus gave rise to hydrodynamics and to astronomy (see illustration #59).[116] The latter enabled philosophers to describe the exact annual path of Mercury as a seven-circuit labyrinth. Incense-labyrinths measured the passage of time (see illustration #61). Scholars thus saw a common link between heavenly and subterranean energies in recognition of the same labyrinthine oscillations in the spiral patterns of flowing water. Numerology, astrology, astrological botany, laboratory alchemy, and geomancy all reflected an inherent (if camouflaged) labyrinth.

The Truth Becomes Straight

Then, when Plato triumphed over Aristotle, science banished the random, the obscure, the complex, and the curved. It sought for the simple, the straight, the predictable. Science looked for causes and found matter as a transparent, orderly, crystalline reality. This new thinking dominated first through geometry, then through mechanics, which furnished models for Kepler and Newton. It triumphed over Renaissance Europe with optics, queen of the sciences, with its marriage of transparency and the straight line, laying the essential physical knowledge for the philosophy of the Age of Enlightenment.

The human body itself was even pictured as a simple machine, made of cogs and levers, straight lines and closed circles. Astronomy and hydrodynamics were dominated by mechanics. In the nineteenth century, the crowning glory of straightness was expressed in the science of thermodynamics, which abolished the reversibility of mechanics, replacing it with the irreversibility the degradation of energy and order. By inventing the notion of entropy, the measure of an ever-increasing disorder, the advocates of thermodynamics definitively did away with any long-term possibility of turning back, negating the blind alley and the bifurcation, the transdimensional shift. Carnot and Lamarck believed they had triumphed over the last remaining vestiges of meandering thought.

The Living Remains Convoluted

However, even during this era the labyrinth remained dominant (and dormant) in an important territory of the universe of science, as well as in that of ideas. First of all, the very construction of a scientific theory is always labyrinthine, with many dead ends and few thoroughfares: error is always a necessary condition of progress. As T.S. Eliot said, "In order to arrive at what you do not know, you must go by a way which is the way of ignorance." Secondly, the labyrinth also serves as a scientific *model*. To the dismay of those who hoped to reconstruct the human body using squares and circles, the discovery of blood circulation led Harvey to abandon the gear-and-lever approach and to represent the body as a labyrinth where life circulates in complex networks (blood, lymphatic, respiratory, nervous, digestive systems), and where blind alleys can be fatal (see illustration #64).

With the Darwinian revolution, the story of life itself was upset, breaking the illusion of the straight line and logical succession of species, and becoming a maze of accidents and interactions, impasses and bifurcations, a labyrinth of innate and acquired influences and a cartography of the fortuitous. Life now advanced by means of extreme detours from simplest to most complex, through a selection of the "fittest"—those most able to survive—which sometimes included organisms whom a handicap had forced towards a supreme effort of environmental adaptation. The link between Darwin and the image of the labyrinth should not surprise those who remember the entire myth— Minos had to look for the "fittest" bull for Poseidon; Aegeus had to send the fourteen "fittest" youths from Athens to be sacrificed at Minos, among whom Theseus was the fittest of all; those who refuse this selection are eliminated; Theseus triumphs abandoning Ariadne and letting his father die. This disappearance of women and the aged might seem to show the labyrinth as favoring the strongest. But the truth of the labyrinth is that, when dealing with gods and the Minotaur, it favors cunning.

We find a similar ambiguity in Marx. Behind the outraged, Manichean dualist, to which Marxists later reduced him, we find a dialectical thinker who realizes that there is no truth that does not contain an aspect of falsehood, and no lie that does not contain its own truth. Rather than the philosopher of the straight line of historical determinism, Marx sometimes takes on the paradoxical appearance of a thinker who introduces the relative and the reversible into a kind of history with no beginning and no end. This is a history without good or evil, gods or laws, where the roads of progress no longer join the avenues of a radiant future, but the uncertain meanders of a History to which humans are subject.

1. Theseus and Ariadne, 15th century © Giraudon.

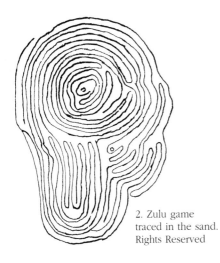

2. Zulu game traced in the sand. Rights Reserved

3. César, The Thumbprint © ADAGP, Paris 1996.

4. Funeral Urn, Italy, Bronze Age.

5. Rock engravings, Pontevedura, Spain. RR

6. Sun Stone,
Savoie, France. RR

7. Neolithic labyrinth,
Val Carmonica, Italy.

8. Stone of New Grange, Ireland. RR

9. Tumulus of Gavrinis, Morbihan, Brittany
© E. Guillemot/Gallimard.

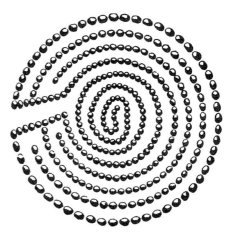

10. Pebble labyrinth, Wier Island, Finland. RR

11. Clay tablet found at Pylos,
Pelloponnesus, circa 1200 B.C. RR

12. Egyptian labyrinth of Athanasius. Kircher, S.J. RR

13. Egyptian hieroglyph
signifying "house," or "palace." RR

14. Tablet for haruspex,
Babylon.

16. Disk of Phaistos,
1900-1700 B.C.
© Lauros-Giraudon.

15. Rhython in the form
of a bull's head, 1500-1400 B.C.
© Lauros-Giraudon.

17. Cretan coins.

18. Cavern of Gortyna,
Crete, drawing by
Sieber, 1821. RR

19. Goddess with serpents,
Crete, 2000-1500 B.C.
© Lauros-Giraudon.

20. Detail from map of Hereford,
13th century, Crete.

21. Ariadne, Theseus,
and the Minotaur,
from a clay vase.

23. Picasso, *Minotaur*,
Vollard suite
© Picasso Estate, 1996.

22. Map of the palace of Minos, Knossos.

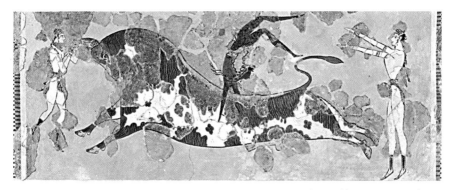

24. Heraklion, *Tauromachy.* RR

25. Brueghel, *Landscape with the Fall of Icarus* © Lauros-Giraudon.

25b. *The Fall of Icarus,* low relief, Hotel du Grand Maitre de France, Musee Vivenel, Compeigne.

27. Roman mosaic, Austria
© E. Lessing/Magnum.

26. Graffiti, House of Lucretius,
Pompeii. RR

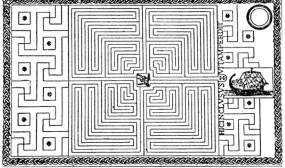

28. Roman mosaic, Tunisia. RR

29. Roman mosaic,
Diomedus' Villa, Pompeii. RR

metain qui tos desuooient ceaus
quila dedens estoient.

en cele maison fu al monstres

30. Life as a labyrinth, from the manuscript of *l'Histoire ancienne jusqu'a César*, 1250 A.D. © B.N.

31. Sans Reparatus of Orléansville, Algeria, 4th century A.D. RR

32. Labyrinth of Crete with Minotaur at center, *l'Histoire ancienne jusqu'a César*, 1250 A.D. Bibl. mun., Dijon, France.

33. City of Jericho, Hebrew manuscript. RR

34. Above, from the Western window rosette of Chartres cathedral © Valoire-Blois.

35. Labyrinth, floor of Chartres cathedral. RR

36. Map of the Chartres labyrinth. RR

38. Map of Chartres cathedral. RR

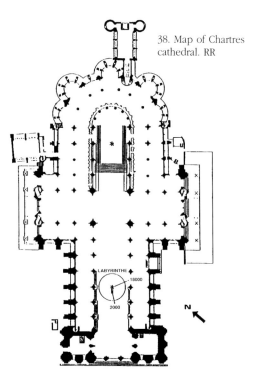

37. The solution of the labyrinth of Poitiers cathedral. RR

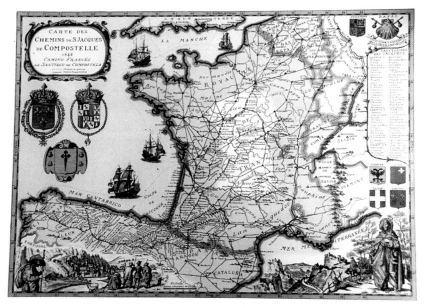

39. 17th century map, *El Camino Francés.* RR

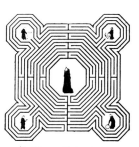

40. Map of labyrinth at Reims. RR

41. Map labyrinth of St. Martin, St-Omer. RR

42. Map labyrinth of St. Vidal, Ravenna. RR

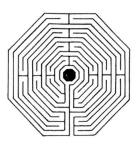

43. Map labyrinth of Amiens. RR

44. Penitents walking on knees through the labyrinth of St. Anne, Nottingham. RR

45. Russian icon, 18th century. RR

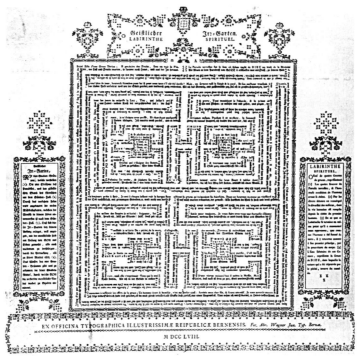

46. French-German bilingual spiritual labyrinth, Berne, 17th century. RR

47. Temporary labyrinth in corn, Reignac-sur-Indre, France, 1996 © Y. Arthus-Bertrand.

PLAN DV
LABIRINTHE
DE VERSAILLES.

48. 16th century labyrinth. RR

49. Versailles, 1674. RR

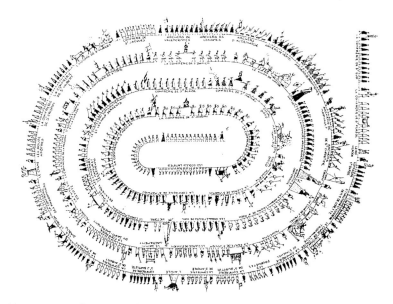

50. Procession of giants, coaches and groups, Ath, Belgium, 18th century. RR

51. Labyrinth from *Alice in Wonderland*. RR

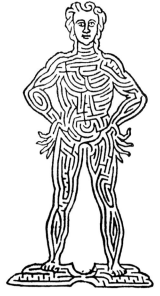

52. Labyrinth man, woodcarving, by Francesco Segala, 16th century. RR

53. The Game of Goose, 19th century, Library of Forney.

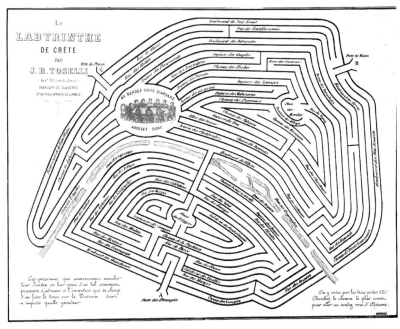

54. "Labyrinth of Crete," paper, 19th century, Library of Forney.

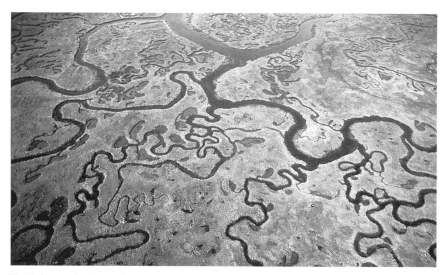

55. Market garden in southern Morocco © Hoa-Qui Agency/Y. Arthus-Bertrand.

56. Moroccan village, Al-Rashidia region © Hoa-Qui Agency/ Y. Arthus-Bertrand.

57. Detail from map of Venice, 17th century © Lauros-Giraudon.

58. Railways © Marc Riboud/Magnum.

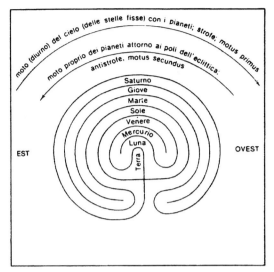

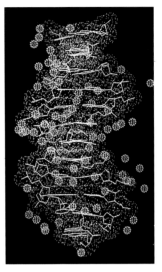

59. The labyrinth as schematic for the orbits of the planets. RR

60. DNA molecule from electron microscope © Cosmos/Oxford Molecular Biophysics Lab.

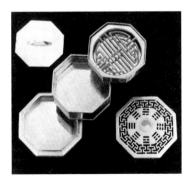

61. Incense burner with yin-yang symbol and divinatory trigrams © Time Museum. RR

62. Cross-section of human brain © Histoire d'aujourd'hui. RR

64. Sectional view of
circulatory system. RR

63. Intertwined serpents,
Navajo sand painting. RR

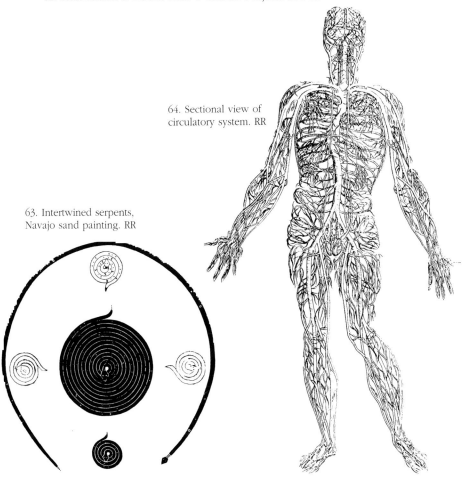

65. Mandala from Rajastan,
18th century, private collection
© *Mandala (Sacred Symbols)*,
Thames & Hudson, 1995.

66. *Le Chateau,*
"European Mandala"
1928, C.G. Jung. RR

68. Humbaba, demon-entrails, Babylon, early second millennium. RR

67. Spider of Nazca, 40 meters long. RR

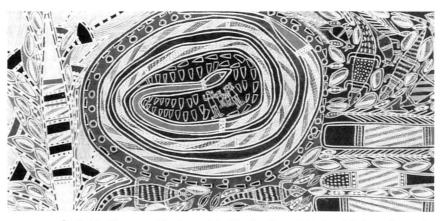

69. Paddy Dhatangu, *The Story of the Wagilag Sisters* © National Gallery of Australia.

70. Hopi symbolism of the Earth Mother. RR

71. Kuba embroidery motifs © Dapper Museum.

72. Drawing to purify the soil. RR

73. Molla cloth from Panama. RR

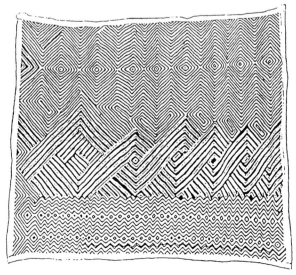

74. Ndengese embroidery
motifs © Dapper Museum.

75. Hopi hunchback
flutist. RR

76. M.C. Escher drawing, *Relativity*. RR

77. Malekula dance, dancer's path. RR

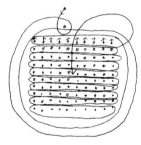

78. Dore Hoyer, drawing by
Johannes Richter, 1968. RR

79. How to draw a labyrinth
© Sig Lonegren *Les Labyrinthes*,
Editions Dangles.

80. The mystical mill,
Vézelay © Zodiaque.

82. *Labyrinthe*, by France de Ranchin. RR

81. Greg Bright, *Maze*. RR

Even more importantly, the figure of the labyrinth has been returning with force in the two major disciplines of mathematics and physics. For one thing, contemporary probability theory employs a labyrinthine mathematics in which a given event no longer has a unique cause nor a fixed logic, where multiple, unequally possible futures exist in a structure of time that has become a labyrinth in itself. Also, the discovery of electromagnetic waves upsets the principles of geometry; a network no longer needs rectilinear efficiency: whatever its form, the time necessary to traverse it remains virtually the same.

Since then, the labyrinth has become an indispensable figure in the sciences. The new non-Euclidean geometries are essentially labyrinthine; and contemporary theories of fractals and oscillations evoke a labyrinth, as does particle physics' use of knotting theory. Probability has invaded matter itself, which is no more seen as a collection of aligned crystals but as an arrangement of fractal labyrinthine spirals whose positions are uncertain, and where everything becomes a complex network of critical paths and dead ends. Nuclear physics, computer science, and even optics—the science par excellence of the straight line— now use labyrinths, either as metaphors or as concrete models. For example, there is nothing more labyrinthine than a printed circuit, whose intersecting connections could never have been designed without the previous advances represented by the transistor, the silicon chip, the pentium chip, or the algorithms involved—themselves vast labyrinths of signs and bifurcations, later generalized as encoded sounds and images. With digital media, every sound and image is the outcome of a labyrinth, an address within a network of forking paths.

Everything in anatomy and physiology is labyrinthine. Fingerprints were long ago noticed to be systems of meanders, each of which is unique to one individual (see illustration #3). The best current representation of the brain is also a labyrinth where complex information circulates (see illustration #62). And the spiral is also found in plants such as the convolvulus, sunflower, and pineapple. Finally, there is the obvious braided helix of DNA itself, labyrinthine source of life (see illustration #60).

Even the Genes

What is the best model for the cell? It turns out to be a labyrinth. In effect, the cell is made up of an array of proteins, which are very long molecules manufactured by genes, which are themselves sections of DNA (see illustration #60). Each cell carries on its functions while confronting impacts from its surroundings. In order to do this, it depends on complex network of about ten thousand proteins, with many different messages being transmitted from inside and from outside. These messages must find their way through the labyrinth of proteins if the cell is to remain healthy. The malfunctioning of certain proteins, whether innate or acquired, sets up barriers to the passage of information, which may interfere with the proper functioning of both cells and organism. Other barriers lead to the volution of new species over time. Even more amazing, if "cell" is replaced by "organism" and "protein" by "cell," the same principle applies: in other words, living beings are labyrinths of labyrinths.[134]

The more path redundancies there are in the protein labyrinth of a cell, the better chance information has to get around possible barriers, and thus the higher the cell's chances of remaining healthy. Since nothing is yet known of the design of these protein pathways (nor of how to read the design of life in the labyrinthine genetic code), research can only seek to identify the places where these barriers might occur. As in guerrilla-warfare strategy, genetic therapy tries to enlarge communication routes so as to prevent barriers being set up, or to find an alternate passage around one if it does occur.[134] Genetic engineering cannot be rectilinear, for it must take into account the multiple possible expressions, suppressions, and pathways of any one allele in the context of dynamically chaning biological fields represented by layers of functional tissue. Thus labyrinthine reasoning is central to the life sciences.

It may be possible in the future to map the overall protein

labyrinth and perform genetic repairs on it but not without recognition of the probabalistic and homeostatic nature of all biological information. Here also, we can find previous remote echoes in myth: through interspecies breeding, the future artisan of genetic labyrinths will give birth to Minotaurs...labyrinthine voyages may even be set up from one species to another, thereby creating a kind of *genetic nomadism* through which humans may be crossed with animals, children conceived of sperm from long-dead individuals. Once again, the "straight line" of lineage gives way to a labyrinth.

Daedalus is the image of tomorrow's scientist, both sculptor, engineer, and labyrinth architect. As practical artisan, she will know the art of metals; as biologist, he will know the future of ants; as artist, her fingers will manipulate all sorts of wax forms; as sailor, he will understand commerce and exchange.

Exchanging

Not only science, but the entire economy itself will become labyrinthine once more.

The First Markets

There is nothing new about the link between market and labyrinth. Crete was already a mobile civilization with vessels that wove vast trade networks which maintained its wealth. This was probably not unrelated to the pride with which Cretans had the labyrinth engraved upon their coins (see illustration #17). In all ancient cultures, ownership itself was labyrinthine—complex kinship rules determined the transmission of ownership—and this still held true in the European feudal system. In the obscurity and confusion of these systems there was profit to be had, and the expert in labyrinths always got the best of the bargain.

Transparency and Profit

Then transparency became the rule: pure exchange should

ideally take place in a linear fashion, with no superfluous intermediaries. Old forms of rent and revenue were banished by the
notion of simple profit from production, without intermediaries.
Property was organized in a simpler, more transparent fashion,
through stockholding companies. The ancient labyrinthine systems of succession were replaced by those of direct transmission, allowing the accumulation of wealth among a limited
number of people. For centuries, Western economies continued
this linear progress of accumulation—at least in theory.

The Return of the Nomadic Economy

Today, the economy is becoming labyrinthine once more.
Industrial and commercial property is melting more and more
into vast tangles of mutual ownership involving financial institutions and holding companies. It is becoming virtually impossi-
ble—except for one who is expert in the labyrinth—to find out
who is the true and ultimate owner of the capital. Production
processes are now diversifying into complex circuits where the
distance between the raw material and the finished product
employs ever more convoluted pathways that are dispersed over
the entire planet. In contrast to the older image of energy being
expended in a linear fashion, information itself circulates in
labyrinths, with knowledge, the main form of wealth necessary
to industry and services, more and more labyrinthine. In particular, knowledge of computer technology—the key to development— is singularly labyrinthine. There is even added value in
the complexity of the labyrinths, and profit depends on it.
Whoever knows how to design, construct, and traverse these,
and obtain information from others' networks, will control profit.

The technocracy that directs large undertakings will organize
itself into labyrinthine flowcharts where operational and functional responsibilities intermingle. Power in such organizations
has already ceased to be pyramidal. Careers are no longer homo-
geneous, nor are they linear and ascending. They consist of ventures, reversals, contingencies, migrations, leaps, impasses,
projections, defeats, and successes. The Daedalus of today might

be a powerful technocrat who designs a financial architecture, a worldwide chain of multimedia stores, a giant computer, or a constellation of digital television channels. He or she might have had to leave a previous position because of patent litigation, or accusations of industrial espionage.

The computerization of working and shopping from home is creating labyrinths where consumers and workers will spend their time. They will look for jobs and many other things in the complex "databases" of these mazes. The media themselves will no longer be transparent networks but sophisticated labyrinths where wealth is to be found precisely in the complexity.

Real consumer goods will become more portable, from telephones to prostheses, and trips will become half work, half tourism. After the pilgrimages of medieval times, the settlement of the New World, the adventures "on the road" of the hippies, as well as their drug trips, we now have the business flights of executives and guided tours of retired people taking their place alongside them as kindred phenomena. Ecotourism brings the wage-earners of the global economy to the rainforests of the Southern Hemisphere, the archipelago of various oceans, the Antarctic ice pack, and even on vacations with Innuit families in Baffinland to share in whale hunts and seal blood. And then, before the exploration of the moons and planets of the Solar System, there is virtual space.

From Wall Street to Frankfurt to Tokyo, stock market traders are abandoning the old graphs in favor of "data landscapes," walking virtually through these labyrinths.

It is not the saving of time that will interest people so much as finding ways to spend it. This means packing a maximum of services into a given space of time. This is exactly like the incense labyrinth, which packs a maximum of time into a reduced space (see illustration #61). In large department stores one already finds multiple entrances and exits, and customers pass through rows of all kinds of merchandise in a labyrinth that has been painstakingly organized for this purpose, with eye-catching displays by vendors and promoters.

Following the superstore model, museum displays are also becoming labyrinthine, with all sorts of exhibits that recall the exotic bazaars and fairs of ancient times. Tomorrow, there will be virtual museums, imaginary reconstructions, collections based on works which are physically spread out all over the planet.

Consumers will walk virtually through direct-sales labyrinths instead of paging through catalogs, which are actually rudimentary precursors of the merchandise labyrinths of the future.

Everywhere, there are signs of the powerful return of the nomadic economy. The future will be one of travel to an extent never known before; first, the very real migrations of marginal and underprivileged workers in search of ever-scarcer jobs; then the virtual travels of the middle classes in search of new distractions, a kind of fantasy tourism; and finally, the quite real voyages of the privileged classes in conquest of new profits. In a capitalism of low inflation and high competition, the deluxe nomads of the future will be armed with liquid capital, no debts or hindrances, and will draw income from a technological situation (knowledge, skills, or opportunities), or control over an innovation in genetics, computer science, investments, performance, or other arts. Possessors of intimate knowledge of the multiple labyrinths of the future, these people will be useful intermediaries or tyrants in the movement and valuation of information in social labyrinths.

The Overclass

These labyrinth masters will constitute an overclass. Their privileges will not be bound to property, nor to means of production, nor to their transmission. They will not be entrepreneurial creators of jobs and collective wealth, nor capitalists exploiting a working class. They will not be administrators, nor owners of factories or real estate. Their wealth will reside in an active and mobile knowledge of the laws of the labyrinth. They will know how to effect a rapid mobilization of both capital and skills in changeable situations, for temporary goals in which governments play no role. Their ambition will not be to direct public affairs (political celebrity would be mostly a plague for them), but to create, to move, to enjoy. They will not bequeath massive fortunes or power to their children. Rich enough to live in luxury, they will often buy hastily and impulsively. Bearers of the best and the worst of the world to come, they will influence society towards fluid values, a carefree attitude towards the future, selfishness and hedonism in their dreams and violence—nomads to the core. The Internet will be their club.

Subject to the laws of this overclass, the middle classes will live a virtual cave-nomadism, in habitations that are both refuges from the world and windows into it. They will settle in there as consumers of virtual voyages of all sorts: work, tourism, games, power, sexuality.

Finally, the poorest, lowliest nomads will be those forced to embark upon the roads of insecurity. Salaries will be eclipsed by temporary work, with everyone looking for the next job offer from a capricious market. Inasmuch as the triumphant overclass floats upon the waters of misery, the success of the few will be paid for by the marginalization of the many, and increasing violence from the underclass. Palestine, Mexico, Indonesia, Albania, Moscow, and Miami offer different present versions of this portent. Tourists and business travelers become prey to marauding bands, urban pirates, and corrupt constabularies. Nigerians conduct banditry via fax, e-mail, and international post. Identity theft has become the newest crime; if the ruling class cannot be deposed, their virtual identities can be coopted.

On the other hand, inasmuch as an open overclass makes its creative skills available in a kind of nomadic solidarity with others, a cultural revolution will take place: that of the labyrinthine economy. It will advocate acceptance of innovation as good news, of insecurity as a value, of instability as an imperative, and of hybrid social mixing as a richness. It will favor the creation of endlessly adaptable tribes of nomads, bearers of original kinds of solidarity. Employment will flourish anew in those areas where labyrinthine skills are being developed. The underclass will be civilized before being enfranchised.

Dominating

The First Powers

In even the earliest human societies, power, like economics, gained legitimacy through a labyrinthine process: the prince's power was derived from his trials and confrontations that echoed the myth of the labyrinth. He was able to channel violence, which reappeared in the sacrifice involved in overcoming the tribulations of the labyrinth. Rulers were recognized and confirmed by their ability to bar the way to subterranean menaces, and to confer meaning upon the voyage towards eternity. So it was that every nine years, the Cretan monarch had to confront the Bull-God alone; if he came out of it alive, he would reign for another nine years.

In Greece, Babylon, India, and Syria, the bull was generally the symbol of a legitimizing threat to power. The Cretan Minotaur, the Babylonian Enkil, the Hebrew Golden Calf: all of them images of a brutal force in defiance of the Prince, yet also legitimizing him. It was also in the form of a bull that the Egyptian Sun-King was reunited with his Moon-Cow; and Jason had to subdue two bulls in order to get to the Golden Fleece.[8] Even today, the bulls' hooves continue to trace labyrinths in the sand of the arena, sometimes stained with blood, confronting the man with the cape and garment of light.

The Twelve Kings of Egypt

The labyrinth also glorified power. When Herodotus marveled at the great labyrinth of Egypt in his second book, he was not only speaking of it as an awesome tomb but as a place of power, built to remind Egyptians of the names of their twelve kings, in celebration of the dodecarchy: "The Egyptians found themselves liberated after the reign of Hephaestus. But, ever incapable of living without a king, they took on twelve of them when Egypt was divided into twelve parts. ...one of their decisions was to have a common monument that would commemorate their names. Once this was decided, they had a labyrinth build above

Lake Moeris, near the city known as Crocodilopolis."⁶⁶ (The twelve tribes of Israel and the Twelve Apostles suggest a strange palimpsest here.) The first great labyrinth thus amounts to a complex structure of imperial authority that forms a labyrinthine hierarchy rather than a pyramidal one, comprising a multiplicity of interlocking regions of power. In Celtic and in Etruscan mythology, the labyrinth also designates a royal tomb, from which the king must be able to emerge to reincarnate. And every prince expects to build one, either as tomb or as garden.

The labyrinth was also a weapon of power, both all-powerful and secluded to protect its secret. Whoever was able to overcome its obstacles was both protected and isolated. According to the historian Philokhoros (c. 270 B.C.), Cretans used it as a prison, when condemnation to work in the mines was still used as punishment. "According to the Cretans, the labyrinth was a prison where the only threat was that of the impossibility of getting out, once one was enclosed there," wrote Plutarch; this was confirmed by Ovid and Virgil.¹⁰² Similar accounts exist in the *Mahabharata,* as well as in Hopi legends.

War as Labyrinth

The labyrinth also contains the greatest secret of military power: the need for strategy to remain opaque. In the Mahabharata, the warrior-priest says: "Today I shall devise an order of battle which is impenetrable even to the gods." Every labyrinth also serves as a rampart, a "sometimes magical defense of a center, a treasure, a meaning."⁴⁰ For example, whether in China and in England, fortifications tend to take the form of labyrinths. Military strategy is always an affair of decoy and misdirection. And in trench warfare, what more perfect labyrinthine form that the networks of trenches, or better yet, the underground defenses such as the Maginot Line or the "Atlantic Wall?" The "Labyrinth" was even a name used for a powerful German position between Rochincourt and Neuvill-Saint-Waast in 1915, conquered at great expense by French troops.

The sovereigns of Europe adopted this military, political, and theological design, building labyrinths where they lived, and their coronations even required the traversal of one such figure. All French kings, except for Louis XVI, passed through the great portal of the cathedral of Reims the day of their coronation, and then traversed the great labyrinth in the nave on their way to the throne. This traversal was so essential that in 1594, Reims being under enemy occupation, Henry IV was crowned at Chartres, so that he could walk the labyrinth there. In 1600, when the Queen entered Avignon, the royal throne was surmounted by a circular labyrinth instead of a fleur-de-lys design.[113]

The Power of the Law

When bourgeois society developed the pretense of power that was no longer apart and isolated from the people, the labyrinth became unnecessary. From this point on, the sovereign began to cultivate the impression that the road of access to him was simple, direct, without manipulation or manners, and open to all. He wanted to encourage all in the hope that they might rise in a straight line into his presence, and even that they might take his place; that everyone born into this world can hope to become anything. That one need only walk straight, following the ideal of order—this was the founding myth of capitalist society in general, and American society in particular.

But all of this in vain—for reality turns out to be quite different in its complexity. The life of the vast majority of citizens leads them into impasses less gratifying than such dreams. Very few are able to emerge into what they call "the light at the end of the tunnel." Very few find the road of access to the royal presence.

Where Political Power Will Be Hidden

Today, power is becoming labyrinthine, like everything else. First of all, no one even knows where it really lies—is there a center or not? A Bastille to be stormed? Who has the power to create jobs? What leadership would be capable of ending fear?

We have passed from the labyrinth of one central power to

that of multiple and changing centers, with powers circulating ceaselessly between them. They protect themselves inside complex mazes where an elusive overclass controls a network of tentacles that are themselves elusive. Democracy itself presupposes the existence of a visible location where power is exercised, a place where "things can be changed," and it is now losing its appeal for lack of a place where it can be exercised. This is what drives exasperated populations into simplistic solutions that are linear, desperately linear.... This is why dictatorships follow dictatorships, tyrannies revolutions.

History itself has become labyrinthine once more. It no longer has a single direction, and it does not necessarily progress towards the good. There is no progress. History is composed of dead ends and disillusion. If any meaning remains in history, it is that of the labyrinth. The "end of history" merely augurs a new beginning.

Future power will reside in the ability to restrict or facilitate circulation on certain paths. Governments can only exercise power through control of networks, and their inability to control them will irreversibly weaken political institutions.

Hence on the Internet, everyone is already trying to protect their own communications systems through the creation of mathematical encryption codes, which themselves are labyrinths involving billions of alternatives to be passed before finding the right access, thus demanding far too long a time for any overseeing power to break the code by systematic trial and error.

War and violence will once more depend upon a labyrinthine art of ruses, detours, the creation of dead ends, and blockages of networks. Terrorism will be exercised above all in attacking power through systems of transportation, computer, and media networks.

Blocking and prohibiting access, transforming avenues into blind alleys, diverting flows of information or movements of people: these will be the characteristics of future power. It will belong to those who know the labyrinth, either because they have built it, because they have a good map of it, or because they have managed to convince others of their competence. This is the power of the *guide:* that of Moses, of initiates, of all those who know how to reorient those who get lost, thereby enabling them to find shelter, land—in other words, to reside.

Residing

The First Cities

When the first cities were born, labyrinths had already structured the habitats of nomadic peoples. Most tribes organized their temporary or seasonal encampments according to skillful, well-thought-out patterns, surrounded by enclosures and shot through with explicitly labyrinthine paths, intended to protect the chief's tent and the sacred altar. Even today, Masai and Zulu tribes live in such provisional habitations, *kraals* (see illustration #2), constructed by women who arrange them in labyrinthine networks with the royal domicile at the center, and complex roads all around it, pre-designed according to a store of mental maps transmitted from generation to generation. The map of the encampment is related to that of battle plans, as protection against attacks by nomads.[84]

The earliest sedentary Neolithic villages, such as those found in at Kaymakli and at Drinkuyu in Turkish Cappadocia, are organized in spontaneous labyrinths made of interconnected cave dwellings.[125] They were able to accommodate twenty thousand inhabitants, and were augmented during later Roman and Arab invasions. Others of this sort are to be found today in Africa, among the Ming and Ping peoples of China, and the Anasazi of North America.

For sedentary peoples, the labyrinth design became a means of preserving the memory of their lost nomadism. They used it as a pattern on the ground to build their villages, to distinguish them from the forest, to trace their place in the structure of the

Cosmos, and to keep savagery at bay by trapping nomads, the enemies of all sedentary peoples.

The first city ramparts were organized like this to slow down invaders' advances. Thus the Bible tells us that the walls of Jericho were labyrinthine; Homer tells us the same concerning those of Troy. As cities grew, their streets naturally came to form labyrinths.

These may even have even have been at the origin of the idea of the Cretan labyrinth; according to Homer, Crete had more than a hundred cities (see illustration #33). One can still see such meandering city streets enclosed by walls in many places all over the world, notably in Uzbekistan, Spain, Albania, Malaysia, and Yemen (see illustration #56). These employ many sorts of protection against strangers, such as great doors that open vertically to the outside by being pulled from the upper stories on a long rope that stretches the entire height of the buildings.

Cities have been labyrinths within labyrinths ever since antiquity. A dead end for one destination might be exactly the right road for another. This permits the stacking and intermingling of an infinity of networks in a limited space. This was also the case with medieval cities, which were more or less intentional labyrinths combining the empty and the full, the wall and the way. Fortified enclosures also defined juridical limits; a major artery nourished and concentrated essential activities, linking the outside to the bell towers of the church. But the complexity of the city afforded even more protection than its ramparts: "The security of a fortified town depends more on the quality of its plan than on the thickness of its walls," the architect Francesco di Giorgio Martini emphasized in his *Treatise on Architecture.* "The city is a cage," affirms Lawrence Durrell's Justine.... In the streets of such cities, the parades of popular festivals and carnivals with giant floats are open-air recurrences of the labyrinthine church processions, and the meanders of the main arteries they follow are touched by a sacred feeling.

The streets guide initiates to their homes, and also allow them to spot any stranger who seems a bit lost and disoriented. Each street is a kind of secret, yet also harbors the hope of an encounter. Prague, and Paris's Ile de la Cité and Ile-Saint-Louis, as well as certain Piedmontese city centers, are among the most beautiful of such labyrinths; the watery labyrinth of Venice is surely the purest among them (see illustration #57).[32] In Lyon, Salzburg, around the oval court of Nantes, or the *Mortier d'or* of Troyes, in Milan, Prague, or a hundred other old cities, we find this occult urban network, known as *traboules* in Lyon, *vicini* in Italy, composed of canals in one place, semiprivate alleys in another, dissimulated in the form of islands, quarters, neighborhoods, ramifications—not being able to find one's way there is always the mark of the stranger.

Addresses and Maps

Then the city slowly became less and less labyrinthine. The passion for transparency drove urban planners to set up an indexing system. Maps and signs carefully named all streets and numbered all houses, with a special name for the grandest ones. For the literate, the labyrinth no longer existed; from this time on, the urban labyrinth could be said to be absolute for the uneducated stranger, but only relative for anyone who could read.

From Renaissance times on, city maps were drawn to scale and sold. Furthermore, streets and plazas were now traced out on paper before being built. The architect was no longer a builder himself, but an artist to be judged by his sketches before the edifice was constructed.

Political power, which more and more espoused transparency, order, hygiene, and defense of property, chased away beggars, strangers, vagabonds—all those deficient in knowledge.[3]

From Haussmann to Le Corbusier

The industrial revolution went even further in expelling labyrinths from the city. Now even the illiterate would no longer experience the labyrinth, for the ruling powers now set out to make the city into a rational artifact. Old winding streets would be destroyed, with new intersections at right angles following a checkerboard pattern and with buildings rising higher and higher. Avenues would be widened to prevent any barricade or traffic jam, the urban arteriosclerosis. Having rid themselves of the poor, the authorities now began to erase the meanders. In France, Baron Haussmann was the theoretician and building contractor of this urban revolution. The city ideal could no longer accept a tangle of tiny streets and byways, for it aspired towards a network of well-labeled arteries and spacious building façades opening onto boulevards where fast-moving traffic—first horse-carriages, then tramways, then automobiles—would soon massively invade the city.

Such designs were easiest to effect where new cities were being built: first of all in North America, where checkerboard cities sprang up out of nowhere. Washington, New York, Chicago, and Houston represent the world's primary antilabyrinthine cities. It is worth noting the declarations of the French architect who was appointed to redesign the American capital: his dream was to lay out clear, straight, transparent roads that would link all the institutional locations of the new democratic power. In 1930, the "Charter of Athens" went even further in this will towards orderliness, and its major ideologue, the French architect Le Corbusier, stated that "The right angle is legitimate...; moreover, it is obligatory." He explained that a city must be linear, with a central artery to which all communications are connected, and around which light is distributed.

Thus these new cities sprang into being, whether functional suburbs like Cergy in France, or fantasy capitals like Brasilia. They continue to be erected today in upscale developments in America and Asia, such as Shanghai's Pudong area.

Cities of the Future

However, since life is not composed of straight lines, even the most artificial cities have never been able to rid themselves entirely of the labyrinth. The growth of a neighborhood is never the outcome of planning, but of a complex reality, imagined by a multitude of players, which is infallibly labyrinthine.[11] In some of the most opulent areas of Europe and the United States, labyrinthine, artificially aged residential developments are being constructed.

Tokyo is the most perfect example today of a labyrinth city, because it has never adopted a sign system. Streets and intersections are without names, and property lots carry numbers that have no relation to those next door. The city has neighborhoods, stairways, and freeways all jumbled together. It is a labyrinth even for its own inhabitants.

Seoul is yet another example of this, suggesting that Asia is the place of predilection for it—as if at least some Asians could not live without maintaining this surplus of ancient memory— and of ancient courtesy as well, required of those who must ask their way. Old maps of Seoul equally resemble calligraphies, Buddhist mandalas, fairy-tale illustrations, and charts of molecular reactions.

Memory and courtesy are conditions of survival for the nomad, and for that of the future inhabitants of great urban labyrinths.

Bordering the great metropolis, the denizens of the suburbs live in their area as in an impasse, where the city center is the forbidden sanctuary.* The most marginal of these people, new involuntary nomads, find their own labyrinths of refuge in unused subway stations, under freeway interchanges, near train stations, in public parks and filthy vacant lots, construction sites, and even in the sewers.

But everyone, from the richest to the most deprived, searches in one way or another through the vast urban labyrinth for some protection, some niche, some defense against the intrusion of strangers, against the aggression of the poor, the arrogance of the rich, the repression of the police, and, in the most elemen-

---

* Translator's note: this refers to the city/suburb relationship in France, especially Paris, which is almost exactly the opposite of that in the United States: a prestigious, historic, high-rent metropolitan center reserved mostly for the privileged classes, and many newer suburbs in social decay, breeding grounds of crime and drug addiction, though the U.S. is now beginning to "catch up" in this regard.

tary and ancient sense, protection from the risks and calamities of nature itself.

It is a safe bet that tomorrow will bring ever more labyrinthine urban structures. Half the population of the planet will be living in cities of over five million, and people will perforce be crowded more and more into spaces that are less and less expandable.[125]

The city will take on a new thickness, as both undergrounds and heights are organized into multidimensional labyrinths, with layers of subway lines and platforms, freeways, light wells, hanging gardens, and all manner of networks, where water, energy, heating, cooling, words, images, money, and messages circulate. Already in China, dozens of cities have doubled their effective area by making use of a network of tunnels, originally built as protection against nuclear war, which bear the same names as the streets above them on the surface. Likewise, in Vietnam, one finds military passageways dug during the war, forming a network of several hundred kilometers and now flourishing with spaces for meetings, health care, eating, and sleeping. Beneath the crowded streets of Osaka, one finds three levels of offices and markets, an entire other city built for peaceful purposes. At the entrance to Shinjuku station in Tokyo, a three-dimensional square figure forms a prophetic emblem of this future. In Montreal and Toronto, where severe winter weather can paralyze urban life, subterranean networks of streets with stores, restaurants and train stations afford an interior life that is well policed and exempt from crime and indigence.

There are other northern cities where three-dimensional labyrinths recreate exotic climates with subtropical vegetation, Polynesian-style pools, and the conditions of an artificial eternal springtime, where middle-class citizens come to amuse themselves in a kind of hometown, quasi-virtual nomadism.

Those who know how to find their way in such cities will have power—primarily the power to communicate.

Communicating

The First Writings

As we have seen, the labyrinth was the original writing, one of the first ways to communicate other than by sounds. In Egypt, the structure of language is represented in the form of a net that traps meanings in order to unite words and things.[30] In Greece the labyrinth was placed under the protection of Hermes, god of versatility, redundancy, dance, and communication. In all societies of that time, communication was indirect and tortuous, requiring intermediaries to whom everyone told their own version of the same story. Priests, bards, storytellers, ecstatics, Griots, prophets, evangelists, all participated in the creation of messages by transposing and representing them. There is nothing more labyrinthine than rumor and word-of-mouth.

Straight Talk

Along with mercantile society came the straight and clear ideal of communication and exchange. Printing did away with storytellers, who could recite a text to which few or none had access. Thanks to books, the text of an author is received directly, without alteration. Letter and spirit coincide, inspiring a briefer and clearer style of writing, banishing ambiguity, rhetorical flourishes, and improvisation. At the same time, Protestantism declared that the priest was no longer an essential intermediary in the reading of Scripture.

The pursuit of speed and the shortest path became an obsession. With automobiles, railroads, and finally airplanes, linearity and transparence became the organizing principles of progress in communications. The communicator becomes eclipsed by the medium. Television is the final stage of this evolution, suppressing all intermediaries in the transmission of messages.

Irrigation Canals

Yet even here, as elsewhere, the labyrinth is returning.

Communication is becoming a form of *irrigation,* with maximum invasion of space by a branching network. It is a remarkable paradox that this nomadic invention has even become indispensable to modern sedentary agriculture, and this agricultural metaphor is the best illustration of the new civilization: the nomad as irrigator of time.

The rule of the straight line received a blow with the appearance of electricity, for which the shortest path is no longer necessarily the best. The most convoluted networks became economically advantageous. Soon after, the appearance of the telephone shook the social order by creating a relationship of equality between communicators. In this new kind of labyrinth, each chooses his own bifurcations in advance by the simple act of dialing. And here also, the straight line no longer rules today, with portable telephones acting as a kind of thread of Ariadne for new urban nomads, and answering machines and voice mail serving to render them "reachable" or "unreachable" for others in search of them.

Internet Labyrinths

In the near future, communications will be fully reconciled to the labyrinth. Television, transportation, and the countless shopping and business networks are like mazes already. Freeways themselves will cease to obey the straight line, which causes more traffic jams as well as accidents due to drowsiness; mazes that multiply road choices between one point and another actually improve circulation. Already, today's freeways are becoming mazes superimposed on one another, with express lanes, interchanges, and one-way access roads. The most effective subway transport systems have multiple redundant maps.

Most future communication will consist of connecting individuals, libraries, and neighborhoods. The return of the labyrinth to communications really began with the 1965 invention of hypertext, a computerized procedure created to allow transit from one text area to another on a screen without one's having to pass through all the passages in between. This permitted a kind of traveling in the text—adding pages, cutting, pasting, creating links between passages. Hypertext's inventor, Ted Nelson, had a dream of linking up all existing texts in a vast structure, like the absolute library envisioned by Jorge Luis Borges.[15]

The year 1969 saw the birth of what would later become the Internet, misleadingly known as the "information superhighway" connecting computers with one another. Two American engineers, Cerf and Kahn, designed communication protocols (known as TCP and IP) for labyrinthine networks, allowing unlimited creation of extra "roads" and addresses in their first computer link. In 1980 the system became public. In 1991, the Gopher system allowed the creation of "tunnels," linking places in a labyrinth with no direct connection between them. At the same time, the Worldwide Web appeared, with its explicit debt to a spider's labyrinth. Instead of linear connections, it used overlapping, interlinked alleys and driveways, thousands of roads that were sometimes dead ends, other times entrances into unexpected encounters. Exactly like older cities, the Internet came to resemble a medieval habitation pattern without a chief architect. Instead of drawing on the principle of the nearest route, it organized treelike paths that resulted in wandering simulations and electronic street-mazes.

It was the familiar metaphor of linear progress that inspired the "information superhighway" notion in the lazy minds that attempted to name the embryonic multimedia networks. But the Internet is actually a labyrinth of information potentially directed to a limitless number of bifurcations, destinations, and users connected to its libraries and databanks. The goal of the voyage is no longer to save time and energy, but to produce and transmit as clearly as possible the maximum amount of information with the maximum ease of access. The simplest path is no longer the best, and the shortest is no longer the most appropriate. The software needed to navigate there will attempt to solve the same types of problems that arise in a labyrinth.

Once it unites with the computer and with virtual-image distribution, television will no longer be a passive spectacle. The

Internet will be the essential communication tool of the future for the virtual nomads, connecting them to all the computers and memories on the planet. They will talk, play, work, seduce, amuse, and consume there. Each person will choose a real or virtual identity for communication. Compulsive lying and schizophrenia will be like masks that are viewed with tolerance in this media carnival. *Everyone will be able to choose who they are, before choosing the person they want to communicate with— or learn with.*

Learning

For most of human history, education and initiation were inseparably joined. Apprenticeship was naturally presented as a labyrinthine passage, with ordeals, masks, and menaces. In Crete, among the Hopis or the Bambaras, and at Ceram in the Moluccas, initiation was the culmination of a sound labyrinthine education. Teacher and priest were one, as were faith and knowledge. Initiation into adulthood conferred the right to live and to pray as a member of the community.

Much later, learning acquired a different meaning, becoming an accumulation of demystified knowledge. Regardless of the age or social class involved, this learning followed a rectilinear path from ignorance to knowledge. Success came to be measured by the number of years of study, and examinations or competitions controlled the right to graduation. This new education conferred the lifelong privilege of membership in a profession, or at least a social status—in theory. But in reality, real knowledge remained labyrinthine, its acquisition complex and tortuous. The number of hours spent in learning still did not provide a true measure of it. Even today, a diploma is no longer a guarantee of employment. Along with everything else, knowledge itself has become precarious, often obsolete as soon as it is acquired. Now our educational systems are becoming labyrinths once again, with complex, nonlinear curricula containing options, bridges, repetitions, and turnabouts. Employment goes to those who have best understood how to find a path, rather than to those who forge straight ahead.

In the future, success will depend on our capacity to navigate, experiment, and persevere. This will demand skills quite different from those employed in the securing of a diploma once and for all. These will include a constant relearning, a returning to the role of apprentice that one imagined was left far behind. We must be able to find value in defeats, to take advantage of impasses and impossibilities. The real-estate developer one day is the Ayurvedic physician and personal coach the next, having made a bad investment in Colorado and attended holistic-medicine college in New Mexico and on the Internet in the meantime. Today's venture capitalist, with his terminal and modem on a boat docked in an urban marina, is yesterday's college professor and city bureaucrat; on the side he does small carpentry. The teacher of the future will not be an authoritarian master so much as an attentive guide.

Much learning will take place at a distance. In this case, the student will have to undergo a stationary voyage, navigating alone through virtual libraries, finding links along the way between different computer labyrinths.

Learning will involve far more than amassing logical facts. It will demand that we undergo trials, learning how to get lost and how to be alert and ready to pounce upon unexpected information. We must have an attitude of curiosity towards our own mistakes. Apprenticeship will be a voyage, first and foremost. The difference between learning, traveling, and having fun will begin to blur.

Amusing

The First Narratives

It was through the labyrinth, the language of the first stories, that human beings began to talk to each other. Hearing stories was the initial form of amusement, the first escape from the everyday, the first virtual nomadism. All myths were means of distraction, in the sense of not thinking about death, or keeping it at a distance.

To open a book is to enter a labyrinth. To read it is to pass through one.

In fact, every great mythic story is constructed as a narrative of passage through a labyrinth.[109] In all of them, we find an entrance, a path, signposts, obstacles, dead ends, deceptions, reversals, signs, omens, respites, treasures, and promised lands. Such tales do not unfold in linear time. We always find ourselves turning around and having to recall previous episodes, sometimes repeating them. The hero threads a way between luck and ignorance, will and reward, and is caught in inextricable contradictions and confronted with impenetrable defenses. The reader of a labyrinthine tale may take advantage of a birds-eye view of the labyrinth, contemplating it as a whole, running through it in the mind's eye, perhaps even starting at the end. But a tale is best when one elects to follow the path from the inside, running up against the unknown, turning pages as one follows a sharp turn along a road or chooses a fork in a path. The greatest stories are those in which the reader cannot escape, compelled to remain on the inside, following all the meanders, anticipating an arrival when one is actually lost, and dreading being lost when one is actually close to reaching a haven.

Explicitly or implicitly, many tales employ a certain form of labyrinth as a leitmotif. Among the earliest legends of this type are *Gilgamesh,* the *Bhagavad-Gita,* and the *Odyssey* and the *Iliad,* where Ulysses is a "hunted voyager" and Troy a labyrinthine city, invaded by a war machine which is a sort of labyrinth itself , the hollow Trojan Horse.[40] Curiously, the word *troy* appears much later as a synonym for labyrinth, based on an old Latin homonym signifying "arena" or "dancing ground." Six centuries later, the *Aeneid* appears as another labyrinthine story: after wandering from labyrinth to labyrinth, from Crete to Cumae, and coming through quite a few metaphysical meanders as well,

Aeneas finally arrives home—and finds a labyrinth.[109] Chaucer's *Canterbury Tales* was the first novel-like story that invoked the summons of travel, of quest, and of escape.[27] In courtly literature, a narrative of seduction often imitates the traversal of a *labyrinthe d'amour,* with the pleasure of losing oneself, the hope of a tryst, and the intoxication of success.

As Ronsard wrote,

"And take you now my heart which thou doest hold
Within the labyrinth of thy entangled ways."

Forthright Amusement

Of course the straight line did manage to impose its rules upon amusement for a certain time. This happened notably in theater, with its rules of unity of place, time, and action. It also dominated French syntax and prose style with the influences of Malherbe and Boileau, respectively. But these very French schools were mitigated by the simultaneous triumph of Baroque or Romantic influences in other countries—and such opposing trends often existed side by side in the same country among contemporaries.

Vitruvius' mystical geometry, embodying Pythagaro-Platonic arithmetic and numerology, passed through John Dee's magic into the stagecraft of Shakespeare's theater where it provided an architectural geography for the contrivances of *A Midsummer Night's Dream, Cymbeline, A Winter's Tale, Troilus and Cressida,* and *The Tempest.* This landscape is reenacted literally in the modern labyrinth of the "The Phantom of the Opera," who steers a boat through fog behind the operatic scenery and is said to have once built a maze of mirrors for the Shah of Persia. This bit of "history" alone suggests that his construction might be a real thing and not a representation of Christine Daaé's fantasy.

Novels and Tales

Thus the structure of the first modern novels also turned out to be labyrinthine. They described a sort of "voyage of the hunted," as in Don Quixote, which is obviously labyrinthine. Later came *Doctor Faustus, David Copperfield, Les Misérables, The Count of Monte Cristo,*and *Around the World in 80 Days.* The same applies to *Moby Dick,* perhaps the greatest of all these, where the ancient mythic elements (migration, mask, hieroglyph, recursive journey, taxonomy) recur exactly, and to *Alice in Wonderland,* where the labyrinth is expressly employed as a device of initiation and resurrection (see illustration #51). In *The Castle,* Franz Kafka describes Prague as a labyrinth "which will not let us go." The labyrinths of Edwin Muir or Borges are like horror-houses.[76] In Joyce's *Ulysses,* Stephen Dedalus gets lost in the labyrinth of Dublin.

But it is the detective novel that, perhaps more than any other genre, is organized in the form of a labyrinth, with the investigator progressing little by little towards the dark center, where the guilty party is hidden, to bring it into the light of day.

Many children's tales are also labyrinths, often harking back to the most ancient times. For example, the story of *Tom Thumb* has all the ingredients: a forest, a monster, a ruse in the form of a "thread" of pebbles to show the way back, and finally a flight above the labyrinth. Much the same applies to *Snow White, Hansel and Gretel,* or any number of other stories.

Today we see labyrinthine amusements returning everywhere, restoring the original purpose of the maze: to give death a meaning. In societies without a paradise, where the hope of resurrection has become an illusion, such amusements serve to help forget the final voyage. The labyrinth must distract, because it can no longer provide an opening into eternity. This is the place it has come to hold in modern art, especially with the success of the cinema—that art of the room in darkness, a kind of contemporary cavern—which is so often structured by a labyrinthine plot.[107] This applies to such very different films as *The Gold Rush, Metropolis,* Cocteau's *Orpheus, Citizen Kane,* or *Vertigo,* as well as to *The Satyricon, The Shining, The Godfather, The Truman Show,* and many others. In a *Highlander* episode, Duncan is stalked through a hedge maze by a rival.

Amusement's Virtual Voyages

To amuse oneself is to take a virtual voyage. It is to accept a different identity of someone who travels, who goes through a labyrinth full of forking paths, blind alleys, and traps. To distract oneself is to distance oneself, to wear a mask, to become another. Here we encounter a different view of the old Marxist stereotype of "alienation," now promoted to the status of self-transcendence in a utopian modernism.

Tomorrow's distractions promise to become even more labyrinthine. Instead of being a simple spectator at an unfolding spectacle of meanders, we will have a choice among various branching paths. All types of amusement will illustrate this, including gastronomy and eroticism: no longer heading straight for the goal, they will involve postponement, sampling, changes of mind, about-faces, bypasses, repeats, and losing oneself in the delights of virtuosity, subtlety, and refinement of skills, until one finally arrives, almost with regret, at the point of consummation.

Participants in these new amusements will choose their own paths in real games or virtual voyages of rediscovery of the purpose that informed the old labyrinth inlaid upon the floor of the cathedral: the virtual road of self-knowledge.

Knowing Oneself

The Fool and the Sage

"Where art thou?" was God's strange question to Adam. Did He, in His omniscience, not already know the answer to this? Or was the divine intention one of leading mankind upon the quest for the self, seeking oneself in a return to the labyrinth?

For millennia, the path of human self-knowledge had been via the labyrinth. This was the normal human condition, and whoever was ignorant of the labyrinth was a stranger, a noninitiate, excluded from the group. Human beings had to learn the meandering paths in order to be accepted into the clan.

From the Renaissance up to the end of the nineteenth century, moral rectitude became the criterion of mental health, and transparency the hallmark of civic virtue. What distinguished human from animal was the moral capacity to walk upright, to be one's own master. There was no more place for the labyrinth in this scheme, and it was reduced to a metaphor for that which is borderline or crazy. The sage walked straight ahead; the fool went astray, escaped, went off the rails of the right road.

Then came psychoanalysis, which taught people to rediscover their dark side, to enter the caverns of the unconscious, to accept themselves as labyrinthine beings. In spite of this, it would appear that the concept of the labyrinth scarcely occurred to psychoanalysis' founders. Freud only mentioned it in a somewhat anecdotal fashion, as an illustration of the sexual meaning of myths: "For example, the story of the Labyrinth is revealed as a representation of anal birth; the convoluted roads are the intestines, and Ariadne's thread the umbilical cord."[55] But it is clearly the labyrinth itself that underlies and illuminates this reflection as a whole. To paraphrase Lacan, the unconscious is structured like a labyrinth. Yielding secrets unexpectedly, it also blocks pathways, sometimes forever, even though those pathways may be entirely open to an approach that will never be tried.

Femininity as Meandering

But first let us enter the very Freudian territory of sexuality. As symbol of the voyage, the labyrinth brings us back to birth and the uterus, whereas the straight line reminds us of the phallus, fertility. If children retain any image of their nine months in utero, it is that of the maternal labyrinth. Just as the hollow, the cave, and the grotto are associated with the labyrinth, they are also symbols of the mother, of femininity, and fertility. To pass through the labyrinth is to pass through the female sexual organs. Common sexual vocabulary resembles that used for labyrinth transit: penetration, entering, and so on. For the Hopis, the circular labyrinth signifies the Game Mother, the Snake Maiden, who embraces both curved and square forms (see illustration #70). Among certain peoples, the labyrinth is such an overtly sexual image that it is considered to be lewd; sometimes it even appears to contain a kind of incestuous nostalgia.

This sexual, seductive association of the labyrinth is universal. In Egypt, Isis guides the seeker to the center of the labyrinth, where Osiris is found. In Finland and in Sweden, labyrinths figure in "virgin's dances." In Crete, the word *Dapuritijo* in Linear B is associated with Potnia, the aboriginal feminine deity. Gilbert Lascault writes poetically of Ariadne as herself the labyrinth, and claims that her vagina is the entrance where Theseus loses his way: "Any beloved body can become the labyrinth which captivates you and leads you astray, a blend of curves and folds enlivened by caresses, it does not necessarily know what it encircles, what it excites."[84] In many legends it is a woman, rather than a bull, who is to be conquered at the center of the labyrinth. Femininity is also an axis of the Greek myth, for Theseus could not have escaped the labyrinth without Ariadne's love. She is the prize of the labyrinth, yet a mere toy of the man who abandons her at Naxos after taking her virginity, the thread that led him into her interior.

Is woman the unconscious of man? This question is raised by the labyrinth myth. And the answer, in mythic terms, is: Yes— and this unconscious must be confronted and neutralized. Of course, woman and man here are not absolute genders but stages in a journey.

Thousands of other labyrinthine voyages have sexual stakes. Orpheus' quest is as much involved with a woman as is that of Theseus. The motive of the *Iliad* is the reconquest of a woman, Helen, at the center of a labyrinthine fortress. This quest for the feminine is also the theme of myths of Ceram, of Malekula, of the Australian aborigines, and of the Hopis, whose Spider Woman guides people out of the subterranean labyrinth.

A Sexual Quest

Ever since Judaeo-Christian sexual guilt sealed the victory of patriarchal virility, represented by the straight line, the labyrinth has been relegated to a metaphor of shameful luxury, decadent allure, and of woman held at bay. In this sense, one finds it occurring in the work of Petrarch, Dante, and Boccaccio. Following the medieval prose tradition of referring to the female genitalia in a similar way, sixteenth-century French *galante* writers such as Béroald de Verville spoke of the vagina as "the precious labyrinth of voluptuousness"; later, Voltaire spoke of it as "the gentle labyrinth," and Willert de Grécourt of "that beautiful maze."[109]

Dreams and Fantasies

In our time, the labyrinth continues to evoke the many themes of psychoanalysis. First came Freud, whose study of libidinal development and dreams was fundamentally labyrinthine—apropos this, T.S. Eliot had a psychiatrist say: "To speak, is to speak of darkness, of labyrinths, Minotaurs, and of terror." Then came innumerable Freudian variants with their suppressed traumas, projections, cathexes, reaction formations, phobias, and counterphobias, like the trails and switchbacks of a labyrinth. Much later came Laing, whose book entitled *Knots* described obstacles in interpersonal communication as entanglements, impasses, and vicious circles. Lacan spoke of the "Borromean knots" of the unconscious, Reich of the nodules of character armor. Finally, and above all, there was Jung, for whom the myth of the labyrinth is a fundamental archetype of the collective unconscious that appears in mandalas, other sacred art, fairy tales, alchemical operations, and dreams.[77] Here, the labyrinth relates the feminine anima—often represented by a princess imprisoned in a tower—to the masculine *animus,* a protector who comes to deliver her from evil. This enables the *animus* to be reunited with the *anima*—exploring one's own inner labyrinth to know one's meanders and blind alleys, to probe one's personal and cultural origins, and to discover how and where the unconscious wears its mask.

To know oneself as a labyrinth, to accept one's multiplicity in a carnival where everyone chooses his or her own mask, whether ethnic, esthetic, psychological, sexual, or whatever: this is the condition, the key, the password that grants access to the labyrinth and allows one to begin to travel the paths of wisdom.

Traversing

Advice for the Traveler

Standing at the entryway, gazing into the shadowed mouth, the profane and the ignorant only see a tunnel strewn with traps, and with no exit in sight. If they turn away from it, they turn away from the door of life itself. But if they enter, overcoming vertigo, fear, and illusions, if they do not create knots inside themselves, and if they allow themselves to make use of very special skills that are often despised today, they will discover that the illusion is an initiation, that fear makes one stronger, that error makes one grow, that vertigo transfigures. Once initiated, one may even return there again, going further this time and helping others make the journey. Thus one becomes a master of the labyrinth.

If we are to accomplish this, we must forget the virtues so glorified by industrial society: speed, reason, logic, and transparency. We must rediscover those of the ancient maze explorers: perseverance, unhurriedness, curiosity, playfulness, trickery, flexibility, improvisation, and self-mastery. The ancients cultivated such qualities in their children through rites and dances that reminded them that they owed their very survival to the remembrance of their nomadic origins and the virtues of the traveler.

Here I wish to offer a few words of advice to future travelers in the labyrinths that are to come.

Nomadism

When standing at the entrance of today's labyrinths, it first helps to put oneself in the frame of mind of ancient nomads, so

as to have a physical understanding of the nature of these meanders. An apparently dark turn of events is thereby transformed
into a constructive advance, helping us to experience this passage as a liberation, bestowing it with meaning and creativity.
We must learn to rediscover the feeling of tribal voyages and the
rich store of vagabond truths, especially bearing in mind these
four major principles:

First, the nomad must travel lightly. The only type of accu-
mulations favored are ideas, experiences, knowledge, and rela-
tionships—not a wealth of possessions, which is an encumbrance
to travel. Identity must be defined not by a territory to be defended but by a culture, belief-system, or god that is portable, borne
by oneself and by one's tribe. This must be defended, even at
the cost of breaking camp suddenly and moving on. The true
nomad never dies in defense of a land, only in defense of the
right to leave it.

Secondly, it must never be forgotten that the nomad is *hos-
pitable,* courteous, open to others, and attentive to gifts and obligations—for our survival depends upon the hospitality that we
receive in exchange for our life-experience. If we do not leave
good impressions behind us, if we have left a wreckage where
we last passed, then we shall be denied access to the wells.
Contrary to what many stories claim, no one is more civilized
and refined than the nomad. Myths illustrate this principle: the
gods cursed the Athenians for their contempt of the laws of hospitality when they killed Androgeos, the son of Minos. And Minos
himself was killed for his similar sin in making war upon Cocalos,
king of Sicily, because of the latter's hospitality to Daedalus.

The third principle commands us to remember to be *on the
alert*. Nomads' camps are fragile, unprotected by ramparts and
moats. Even when they have chosen an empty, unclaimed place,
even when they have been generous in their hospitality, the
enemy may charge unexpectedly, anywhere, and at any time.
Nomads must always be ready to break camp or to deal with an
enemy emerging from the forest or the desert.

Finally, one must remember the *solidarity* among nomads.

They need each other, traveling companions who share hopes and burdens. A nomadic lifestyle cannot exist without a watch, and the watch must be passed to each in their turn. This requires an organization based upon solidarity.

Lightness, courtesy, alertness, and solidarity: these have been the basic principles of nomads since time immemorial. Travelers must avail themselves of these principles above all, if they are to face up to the challenge of the labyrinth.

Facing Up

Once at the threshold, we must still find the courage to enter. And it does require great courage, for all citizens of modernity fear the labyrinth, accustomed as they are to broad avenues. They are not inclined to advance when they can only see a sharp turn ahead, or a dark and gaping chasm. They feel that once inside, they will be lost and bereft of resources. They have been taught that the labyrinth has swallowed all who entered it: Minos lost his wife, son, and daughter there; Daedalus and Theseus their sons; and Ariadne her love. At Ceram in the Moluccan Islands, in Malekula, in Africa, America, and Australia, all the legends and myths say that this is a place where one becomes lost and dead, encountering only nothingness or the serpent's venom.

This is enough to daunt even the bravest. Why leave the comfort of sedentary life? Why get involved with meanders? Those who hold fast to Reason will refuse to go a step further, for they aspire to security. It is "rights" that they demand, not uncertainties and choices. If choices are imposed upon them, they recoil; they may even go so far as to invoke liberty in order to avoid having to choose.

There are those who will try to circumnavigate the labyrinth. But life does not allow us to avoid going through it. To attempt to do so is a refusal of life—ultimately a form of suicide.

Others will still try to keep to a straight line as they go through life, clearing a straight path by force, as recommended by

Descartes. Mostly, they will fail, for the way of the straight line is useless for anyone who wants to live in the real world. Even Daedalus failed to escape his own labyrinth, and strove to fly out of it. Alexander failed, obtaining only a fugitive victory in his cutting of the Gordian knot. To attempt to get through a city without attention to its plan, to profit from knowledge with no appreciation for how it was acquired, or to rule a country without studying the labyrinths of its ways—all such efforts are doomed to failure.

Still others will step into the labyrinth and then be overcome by fear and try to turn back. The punishment for this is terrible. Similarly, Orpheus braved the labyrinths of Hades to save his beloved, mastering the obstacles of the descent; but when returning, just before leaving, he looked back. This caused him to lose everything he loved, and ultimately to die by being torn to pieces.

Finally, there are those who enter the labyrinth but resign themselves to living indefinitely *inside* one or another of its coils, no longer seeking to get through it, accepting life in this prison rather than venturing outside of it.

But, in contrast to all of these, the only viable attitude is that of entering fully into the labyrinth, facing up to nomadic existence as it is, leaving behind the devices of sedentary life, and seeing the labyrinth as a solution rather than a problem. In order to realize this, one must advance with a willingness to be lost.

Losing Oneself

It was only through becoming lost that Ulysses realized his love for his wife, that Columbus discovered America, and that Newton understood gravitation. The Jews received their Law after becoming lost in the desert. Celtic wisdom refers to this principle: "There are those voyages in which mariners have lost their way, when they stow their oars, when they are no longer going anywhere; and this is when they attain the Blessed Isles."[30]

In industrial society, to be lost is to be a loser—a loser of time, a loser of money. All modern societies see failure, and even madness, in going astray. You are supposed to walk straight ahead, knowing where you are going and never admitting that you are lost.

The labyrinth—including all the labyrinths mentioned here—requires a very different attitude. When we enter it, we must accept disorientation, life outside of familiar space and time, vertigo, dizziness, and lack of advance knowledge of either the way or the time the trip will take. We must accept the possibility that even when we think we are reaching the center, we may in fact be on a path leading us further away from it.

Some languages have understood this well, by associating the word for labyrinth with one meaning *straying*. For example, although German has the word "labyrinth," a more common word is *Irrweg,* or *Irrgaten,* from the verb *irren,* to stray or wander. This root is also used to mean a protector, as if errancy itself could protect. In Old English, "maze" is related to being lost or bewildered, amazed. In Chinese, there are two characters designating the labyrinth, *mi* and *kung,* one of which is associated with going astray, being lost, confused, troubled, fascinated, enchanted, passionate, or madly in love; and the other meaning temple, palace, or womb.

The truth is that *being lost never means defeat.* It is a time for reconsideration, for going where one is not expected to go, for finding oneself. We should even *desire* to go astray, to take pleasure in being lost, transforming our path into one of expectant curiosity instead of struggle and strife. In this way, we do not fear errancy and solitude. We conquer our fear of the unknown, allowing ourselves to advance blindly, even though we know it is possible that an enemy lies crouched and waiting just beyond the next turn. In science, nothing is discovered without straying, and one finds nothing that one does not search for. In art, being lost is the precondition of creation. In apprenticeship, nothing can be learned without the experience of failure.

To enjoy being lost also presumes the special quality of

curiosity. It is what enables us to learn from losing our way, to make discoveries in the unknown, to find something through our ignorance. It means being interested in others, never starting off by imposing our own way, being alert for all kinds of differences, and putting oneself in a stranger's place in order to understand his or her uniqueness. Curiosity is the most vital quality of the nomad and is indispensable for voyagers of the future. There are a number of video games that provide quite good training in this. In such games, I see an exercise that is infinitely richer than the passivity of watching television. It is a curious coincidence that such technology has arrived just in time to demonstrate its initiatory utility for the adolescents of tomorrow.

We really get to know a city by losing ourselves in it. Rabelais called it "labyrinthing"; in the winding streets of Lyon, it was called *trabouler.** It means taking pleasure in getting lost.[32]

On the Internet, it is by getting lost that we find out things that we did not realize we needed to know.

By getting lost in ourselves, we may someday attain self-acceptance.

Accepting Oneself

Citizens of modernity have become oblivious to the splendors of solitude. Society encloses people in a type of network—woven of familial, economic, social, ideological, or religious filaments—that does everything to condition them to dislike being alone and to dislike themselves when they are alone. Solitude is seen as a kind of defeat, like the last stage before death, even as an understandable and legitimate justification for suicide. And the social system does its utmost to fill people's solitude with devices that distract them, or voices that deafen them

---

* Translator's note: The French verb coined by Rabelais is *labyrinther,* literally "to labyrinth." The meanders of the city of Lyon were known as *traboules,* hence the verb *trabouler.*

as they speak. Avoidance of solitude is one of the driving forces of consumerism.

In spite of their mostly tribal lifestyle, with its imperative of solidarity for personal and group survival, nomads find nourishment in solitude. It is the unfailing traveling companion for each and all of them, not only to be tolerated but to be rejoiced in. This is only possible if one accepts oneself fully for who one is—perhaps sometimes with the help of the guiding love of an Ariadne who remains outside....

But the sooner we learn this, the better: the labyrinths of the future will have to be confronted alone. This will require us to accept our own peculiarities with self-tolerance, never judging ourselves by others' opinions of us. We must learn to do what needs to be done with knowledge of how to live with ourselves, to listen to ourselves, love ourselves, without fear of being forgotten by the rest of the world.

The game of the labyrinth can help in such self-recognition. It helps us overcome the disappointments of blind alleys, to discover ourselves with tolerance, to learn to live with our weaknesses, to make ourselves available, to take a small or a giant step towards self-acceptance. This is what gives us the strength to persevere.

Persevering

In Praise of Disappointment

Once we are in the labyrinth, having accepted being lost there and having tasted the joys of solitude, we must still learn to persevere in the face of difficulties, bearing with disappointments and failures and not giving up.

Neither capitalism nor democracy are any help here. Each of these systems has encouraged worship at the altar of impulsive whim. We want to have it all, and we want it now—or at the very least, we expect to have a constant view of the "light at the end of the tunnel." This failing, we abort everything and look for a different plan. Our society has brought precariousness even into desire, capriciousness even into ambition, and it does not prepare us for the challenges of labyrinths.

To traverse the immense meanders of the future, we will have to know how to persevere, accepting failure, not giving up in the face of disappointment, resisting defeatism, and learning how to overlook things—in other words, we must learn detachment and equanimity as we advance in the dark with no certainty of getting anywhere, our inner regard fixed upon an invisible aim, with an ambition organized around a clear mental image of our future.

For nomads, nothing is lost forever, and errors can be corrected. Their discipline is one of taking nourishment from hope, as long as they live, in order to persevere in the voyage. As Christopher Columbus said, in one of his most surprising declarations, "It may be that hope only exists in voyaging."

Greece provides three models of this. Theseus is an example of a kind of political perseverance, in his desire to save Athens from the Cretan curse (his abandonment of Ariadne could be seen as vengeance for his people's humiliation). Ulysses, "the man of a thousand ruses," exemplifies faithful perseverance. For ten years, he sought to get free of the sea in order to return to the woman he loved, resisting the temptations of Calypso, Circe, Nausicaa, and stopping his men's ears with wax in order to block the sirens' song. In spite of his Cretan origin, he has important points in common with Theseus: like him, he was pursued by Poseidon, who tried to drown him; and he also consulted the spirits of the dead, descending to meet Hades, Judge of the Underworlds. Finally, Penelope herself is an example of perseverance: this granddaughter of Poseidon kept her suitors at bay by testing them with a mighty horn-bow, as well as twelve double axes, also symbols of the labyrinth.[47]

To experience the voyage of life to its fullest, like Ulysses; to remain unperturbed by all kinds of threats and terrors, like Theseus; to confront solitude and suffering like Penelope—these are aspects of the virtue of perseverance, involving patience, stubbornness, and determination.

Time Is Part of Space

All these qualities demand a very different relationship to time from that of industrial societies. The very first labyrinths already taught this conception of time, for they were concrete demonstrations of time transformed into space. In water clocks, water labyrinths, incense labyrinths, or even labyrinths of drifting smoke in the air, time is seen to be measured in terms of space. The labyrinth is the mirror-image of the hourglass: the latter is space manifesting within time, and the former, time manifesting within space. Like the hourglass, the labyrinth requires a going and a returning. Like the labyrinth, the hourglass measures a potentially infinite time within an enclosed space.[4]

The labyrinth demands and determines a very special approach to time: it has nothing to do with saving time, but with invading it and spending it. "A lifetime," wrote Seneca to his friend Lucilius, "is the only property a person has. It must be used fully, and to its depths." This is precisely the nomadic philosophy. And this Roman patrician also provides us, very naturally and unwittingly, with the most beautiful possible definition of the labyrinth: *"To create an infinity of paths within this finite space."*[15] Yet this is not some Epicurean ethic of bedazzlement by the narrow present moment, but a filling of all life's time to the maximum, without limits and without impatience.

The time of passage of a nomadic life must be one of time invested, not saved. It is a space filled from top to bottom, not one of future expectation. In fact, the nomad lives outside of time until the oasis is found again—if it is found. Time is not something to be saved, but to be filled to the brim, to be augmented in length and in intensity throughout life.

The labyrinth returns us to a time of taking our time. Here, time piles up, twists around, wanders about and gets lost. It denies urgency. It allows an idea to mature through a process of hesitation and turning back. We do not lose time by persevering; we gain by reflecting before we act. A perseverance that involves trips back and forth, to and from the same goal, is not a quality of the modern "golden boy" but of the wise ones to come, who will know how to make vacillation into a virtue.

The aim of perseverance is not the accumulation of material wealth (which is mostly an encumbrance to the nomad), but of experiences. This implies constantly trying new things. In order to overcome the discouragement this may entail, we must have a goal that goes beyond the immediate moment, an ambition that justifies our effort.

It also implies freedom from time which is ordered by others, so as to find one's own order of time. We can no longer afford to allow ourselves to drift along with the linear passage of the hours, if we are to follow the meanders of our inner path. First and foremost must be the remembering of oneself.

Remembering

Memory or Death

We may go through a labyrinth blindly, and then travel it backwards by sheer chance. But if we want to avoid endless loops, repeating the same mistakes, we must have help. Nomads need signs or guides. And when there is no magic thread to be found, no pebbles, arrows, signs, or maps to be consulted, *they have need of their memory.*

Memory is not something unique to human beings: mice and rats are able to remember the best path in a labyrinth involving ten choices, later avoiding dead ends without hesitation. They are capable of learning how to go around an obstacle. But human beings will need a far more sophisticated memory in order to face up to far more demanding mazes.

Nomads have always known how to cultivate memory in dealing with multiple labyrinths—not only because they need to remember the right road and the location of the oasis, tree, or rock that serves as a landmark, but also because they must avoid carrying burdensome objects and must remember the locations of a maximum number of technically useful objects when they become necessary. Their wealth is not measured by what they carry, except in their heads.

Nomadic identity is not defined by a territory. It is not evoked by gazing upon a landscape, visiting a cemetery, nor lingering in a house. Nomadic roots are found in stories, songs, dances, ceremonies, and techniques, and especially in a God who is also nomadic, accompanying one everywhere. Such a God is necessarily unique and universal, the nomad's first memory and primal certainty, promising a Land in which to set down one's baggage. The labyrinth helps the nomad to escape from polytheism, even while remembering it: "Remember that you were once a slave in the land of Egypt." (Deuteronomy 22-24)

The nomad cannot even take the risk of distributing all of memory's precious stores among different members of the tribe, because one never knows when the group may disperse. Nothing can be absolutely delegated to others. Also, the nomad has neither priests nor masters. Maintaining one's own memory intact is a matter of life and death. This helps to endure one's solitude, to avoid repeating the same mistakes…and when one has finally plumbed the depths of the labyrinth's mysteries, he (or she) is made an initiate.

Learning by Heart

There are many cultures in which memory training is an essential element of adolescent initiation. Often, the exercise consists of memorizing the design of labyrinths. This occurs from Africa to Polynesia. In Tibet, the *nahal,* the *kulam,* or the *mandala* were favored as means of memory training. In ancient Europe, labyrinths were used to memorize texts, especially poems, which themselves can be seen as labyrinths, studded with rhymes as guideposts. In those days, in order to have full access to a text of which very few copies existed, the only possible private library (except for clergy and aristocracy) was that of memory.[131]

Greeks and Romans exercised memory by visualizing a labyrinth, and associating each corridor, each turn, and room, with a portion of the text to be memorized. This *ars memorativa,* with its special techniques, formed an entire literary subject in itself.[131] For example, Cicero explained how a person with this kind of literacy might learn to attain full recall of a mental labyrinth several leagues long.

This link between memory and labyrinth deserves deeper study. Anyone who examines scientific pictures of the brain can sense that memory must have something labyrinthine in its structure (see illustration #62). Saint Augustine, in his *Confessions,* gave a superb description of memory as a succession of caves. This text is worth quoting at some length: "And now I arrive in the estates and vast palaces of memory, where the treasures of countless images are to be found, brought there by drawing them forth from all perceived things…. There I also encounter all that has been deposited and stored in reserve, and that has not yet been drowned and buried by forgetfulness…. In the plains, the grottos, and the incalculably vast caverns of my memory, incalculably full of an incalculable number of things…through all of these things I run, I fly, I plunge in this and that direction, as deeply as I desire, never finding any limit."[131] For Augustine, God may also be sought in this labyrinth of memory: "You have done my memory the honor of residing there, but in what zone of it do You dwell? This is what I ask myself. In thinking of You, I forsake the zones where the beasts reside, for I could never find You in the midst of corporeal things. And I came into the zones to which I had consigned the feelings of my mind, and I did not find You there; I entered into the very seat of my mind, yet I did find You there either. Why search any further for the place You dwell? As if there could be any such place there…. There is no place; we advance, we retreat, and there is no place…." This is a magnificent description of the various "quarters" in the labyrinth of the mind, a true precursor of psychoanalysis. But it also records the failure of the quest for God as dwelling in memory; "He" is rather a lack in memory, an *absence.*

Throughout the Middle Ages, other writers continued to cite the labyrinth as a mnemonic device. For example, Albert the Great recommended making use of existing edifices as "effective" mental labyrinths.[131] He explained that there was no need of inventing a fictional labyrinth, since one can recall to memory an actual building one knows—preferably a religious one of course—and associate each portion of the texts one wishes to memorize with various locations there. He claimed to have learned the entire *Summa Theologica* of St. Thomas Aquinas by heart in this way, by locating each part of it in a particular place in Chartres, a Gothic cathedral with which he was thoroughly familiar.

After him, other theoreticians further elaborated this art of memory, including Giordano Bruno, in *De Imaginum Signorum et Idearum Compositione,* a book written shortly before his execution. In this, he visualized an amazingly sophisticated system of rooms, each arranged according to a kind of magical geometry, distributing the *wings of memory* among four rooms, each of them divided into nine places of memory, which were each further composed of fifteen *campi,* themselves subdivided into nine places and thirty *cubiculae,* and so on....

This kind of demand upon memory disappeared along with the world of the labyrinth in general. Having become sedentary, our travelers now saw fit to get rid of encumbrances to memory, storing wisdom, then culture, then knowledge outside of themselves. In this way, they began to consult the memories of the ancients, of priests and of masters; then of books, files, and finally of computers.

Such amnesia is even necessary to the smooth functioning of a capitalist economy—it not only offers a perfect pretext for commercializing the things being stored, it also makes them obsolescent and devaluable when the memory of their true worth is lost. Memory is the enemy of salesmanship. The circulation of goods and capital is propelled by cranking out new fashions and endless hit-parades. Hence everything is done to absolve consumers of any effort of memory: signs, maps, catalogs, labels, manuals, as well as libraries and computers, aim to rid human beings of the bother of having to remember.

The Future of Memory

Today the need is being felt for a nomadic kind of memory that will enliven ours once again, as we navigate through cities, schools, work, and the Internet. But also we need it in order to have a sense of belonging—all identity is cultural, and belonging to a tribe presupposes a common culture: a transmitted memory.

Memory is also essential to creation, a means of extending new bridges between unrelated things. Just as we must know many facts relating to a great number of fields in order to set up new links between them when the time is right, so in the future we will have to know many networks, memorizing a number of algorithms and paths, in order to navigate the labyrinths of labyrinths, advancing ever further into them without having to undertake endless searches.

The most handicapped and excluded victims of tomorrow will be the amnesiacs, both absolute and relative, who are unable to deal with labyrinths, who require and demand the literal, the calibrated, the alphabetical.

The exercise of memory would suggest a return to fashion of forgotten and discredited exercises of the past: learning by heart, retaining details, playing memory games, and so on. This is surely one of the great virtues of video games, which might serve to reassure anxious parents of children who seem to waste entire afternoons playing them.

At school and at home, it will be necessary to relearn the arts of memory with the help of labyrinths. But beyond this is the need to imprint memory in the body—to dance.

Dancing

The memory of a path inscribes itself more effectively in the body than in the mind. This is the beginning of the art of the dance, a strange place of meeting between a very ancient image and one of the major talents of the future, one of the paths of wisdom.

To dance is to move along the lines of a labyrinth. All myths teach that the labyrinth is the origin of the dance.

Theseus Invented the Dance

After fleeing Crete and abandoning Ariadne at Naxos, Theseus and his companions engaged in a circle-dance, one in front of the other, "with a combination of alternating, circular movements," around the altar of Apollo.[102] The dance evoked Ariadne's thread, the twists and turns of the labyrinth, and the courtship dance of the male stork, also taught by Ariadne. It took place upon a dancing ground originally designed by Daedalus at Knossos. Theseus thus expressed his joy at being delivered from the trap, and at having conquered the Minotaur. This dance of initiation and divination continued to be practiced for centuries on the island of Delos, and at Athens during the Oschophoria festival. Eustace wrote that "the seven young men and virgins who were freed from the labyrinth along with Theseus performed this dance for the first time near Knossos, led by Daedalus…and there are many even today, especially sailors, who still stop there to visit the cavern, performing an interlocked dance full of turns, which they believe to be an imitation of the convolutions of the labyrinth."[114]

Processions and Corridas

This connection between dance and labyrinth is found everywhere (see illustration #77). The Trojans danced around the tomb of Anchises, imitating the serpent that emerges regularly from the tomb. The builders of Roman cities continued to practice an inaugural dance of this type. Traces of such labyrinthine processions are found in Assur and also in Babylon, where a labyrinth was often used as an arena in which a dancer mimed the motions of the Sun. At Ceram, a spiral dance evoked the murder of Heinwele, the girl who was buried alive. At Malekula in Celebes, the dance is a very important exercise of remembrance of the designs of the *nahals,* a necessary condition for access to eternity. Among the Zuni and Hopi Amerindian tribes, spiral dances are performed during the great winter solstice festival, with serpents playing a major role. For the Mayans, a spiral was the symbol of the winter solstice, with a dance offered up to the Sun, for strength to begin the year again. The same features are found in African initiation ceremonies, as well as among the Australian aborigines, where every initiate must be a choreographer, painter...and a great lover.[8] In Egypt, this kind of choreography is executed during the sacrifice of the sacred bull in place of the King. In Palestine, a dance known as the "partridge" is performed in honor of the Moon Goddess, under the name of *pessech,* which means "the limping of the partridge" (the same bird that the prophet Jeremiah used as a warning symbol).[28] In Rome, Virgil wrote that the dancers "weave" their movements. A dance like this also came to Brittany, brought there by eastern Mediterranean invaders at the same time as Celtic labyrinths began to appear in the Bronze Age, as did those of Sweden, Russia, and Italy, which also served as dancing grounds.[119]

Dance is always and everywhere a source of liberation (see illustration #78), ecstasy, the exaltation of the body, and communication with the beyond. This form of prayer is practiced among the dervishes of Islam, as well as the Hassidic Jews of Eastern Europe, whose dance is a supplement, sometimes even a substitute for prayer: "Every day one must dance, at least in one's thought," as the great theologian, Rabbi Nachman of Breslau so magnificently proclaimed.[94] In the same spirit, he might well have recommended contemplating a labyrinth, traversing it in one's thought so as to free oneself from the world's anxieties.

It has been often observed that the bullfight is also the descendant of the labyrinth and the dance of initiation. The bull is the Minotaur, pursued through a labyrinth in the city, before erupting into the arena. The final phase of the ritual of the corrida represents the meeting with the monster, the combat between the prince and the bull, the sacrificial dance. The arena is the center of the labyrinth. All the steps performed there form a choreography. They fascinate the spectators, whose admission to this place permits them to witness one of the most closely guarded secrets of ancient times: the Prince's trial and moment of truth, the combat-dance of power and of death.

Like all sacred arts, the dance later devolved from ceremony to spectacle. This tends to reduce the labyrinth to a simple mental pattern to guide dancers, a choreographer's work diagram.

Distinguishing the Body

The current return of the labyrinth is also an unprecedented inducement to rediscover the virtues of dance. This explains the growing fashion of mastery of the body, like a master training a pupil, so that the body can serve one's personal growth.

For a dancer cannot be reduced to his or her body. The body is even external to the dancer, a partner in a dialogue, continually being commanded to move elsewhere. Like the voyager in the labyrinth, the dancer must first possess self-acceptance and perseverance. The dancer also dies symbolically, traveling to the realm of the dead to return as an initiate. Maurice Béjart declares that "the dance unifies time and space," and is a means of "making the body an ally of the spirit." It links thought to movement, liberating and elevating the dancer, who must strive to the utmost to find the path by which his or her body will lose its heaviness, becoming lighter and hence more nomadic. In order to achieve this, the dancer must master and minimize all superfluous movements, freeing one's roots from the ground, weaving one's own path, circulating air through the body like a labyrinth, turning like a helix that rises away from the earth. Then purity of gesture can stream forth from the corporeal labyrinth, invading space in its fullness and occupying it totally.

The dance is therefore the art of identifying one's body, of perceiving what happens to it as something external to oneself, whether pleasurable or painful. To be out of one's body—this is the paradoxical reality of the dance. It leads us to go out of ourselves, to get free of the miasma of the viscera. This means that one must also agree to become one's own representation in order to have the capacity to live in a kind of carnival that is external to one's body and one's gestures: to be another. Here again, we find the confirmation of the relation between mask and labyrinth.

There are other movement traditions besides dance, which also return us to labyrinthine forms and going outside ourselves, such as chant, mime, yoga, aikido, t'ai chi ch'uan, shintaido, reiki, crainal osteopathy, contact improvisation, and so on. Each of these teaches the science of gesture and distancing of the body in its own way, by remembering oneself—and by playing. Each elicits an intuitive anatomy that defies simples locations and repertoires of skeletal, visceral, or neuromuscular elements. In the Brazilian martial art of capoeira developed by African slaves, opponents fight using their feet as hands, their hands as feet, all the time dancing within a circle called a *roda* to the music of the *berimbau*—and this sparring is called "playing."

Playing

The First Games

A labyrinth is not only a metaphor for ritual or transcendence—it is also a playful enigma. While our world is more and more invaded by labyrinthine complications, this also means that life is there to be lived fully, in gratuitous freedom and nonviolence, like a game that enables us to escape the very anguish it involves.

Playing a game is not an innocent activity. Games reach back to the dawn of time and have their source in the sacred. Most of them originate in ritual ceremonies and religious apprenticeships.[22] For example, Hopi children learn rites and are initiated into world-creation narratives by means of games that mime these myths, and also by means of kachinas, wooden dolls that serve as spirit images.

All over the world, we find labyrinths as religious games. They instructed people in the designs that the spirits would require them to recognize at the moment of the Great Passage. Thus at Malekula, people constantly played at drawing *nahals* so as not to forget them when the time came to face the spirit of Death. Similarly, the Zulus still enjoy improvising drawings of labyrinths in the dirt, called *usogexe,* after smoking cannabis. The author of a labyrinth challenges the other players to attain the "royal abode" at the center. When a player fails to do so, the others cry, *"Waputra usogexe!"* ("The labyrinth really got you!") The game begins over and again, continuing for hours, and hashish smoke is blown back and forth as if to represent spoken words. Here again, the labyrinth appears as a kind of substitute for language.[30] The neighboring Cafres also challenge each other with labyrinths drawn in the dust. And the same kind of game is found among the Pimas of Arizona, serving also as an apprenticeship for metaphysical labyrinths.[14]

Sacred games and labyrinths elicit the same feelings of simulation and vertigo.[22] "That which is sought through hardship is found with the greatest pleasure," as Saint Augustine noted. This is true regardless of whether it is a quest for the gods, for God, for supreme value, or for the source of ecstasy or beatitude.

Much later, church and garden labyrinths also became games, and simulations of apprenticeship in matters of sin, grace, and resurrection.

Hopscotch and the Game of Goose

Finally, labyrinths and mirror-mazes began to appear in fairs and amusement parks, openly touted as places of pleasure. The first amusement park, the Crystal Palace at Sydenham, which opened in 1850, had a labyrinth that enjoyed an immense success.[126] Players experienced all the thrills of simulated terror, vertigo, disorientation, fear, and relief. The same sensations were offered more recently in attractions such as the "Wooz" (Wild and Original Object with Zoom) in Japan and the United States. Some of these amusement labyrinths effect distortions (another means of becoming "other"), and some also change their form while one is going through them. In any case, they are typically the major attraction in such parks.

These games recur in the form of puzzles for children or adults, appearing in newspapers or books. Some of them are especially subtle and difficult, such as those of France de Ranchin or Greg Bright (see illustrations #81 and #82).[17]

There is an entire category of games that, like the labyrinth, structure a passage along a complex path beset with obstacles, which can require going back, sometimes to the starting square. These games I shall call "labyrinthic," to distinguish them from "rectilinear" games, which involve progressing as quickly as possible along a path without such complications.

The layout of hopscotch is undoubtedly the most ancient form of these labyrinthic games. It involves a trajectory where one risks getting stuck, between a "hell" and a "heaven." The most ancient known game of this type dates from the fourth millennium B.C. in Egypt, in the place now known as El Mahaswa. Numerous other examples have been found in Crete, Rome, Greece, India, Russia, China, and Latin America. The most primitive take the form of labyrinths or "snail shell" spirals. Later they influenced the form of church naves.

A related game called *Senet* was discovered in Egyptian tombs, which the dead were supposed to play for access to the gods. From the Ivory Coast comes the related game of *Awele,* where players must follow two lines of pebbles, with dead ends and turnabouts.

Another very famous labyrinthic game is the game of goose.[*] According to legend, it originated in the Greek army during the siege of Troy, serving to teach patience and strategy to the troops.[122] It reappeared at the end of the fifteenth century in the form of a spiral divided into squares, some of them dead ends, and others forcing a turnaround. Fourteen of these squares represented the geese (also the number of youth sacrificed to the

---

[*] Translator's note: the French board game is *le jeu de l'oie,* called "the game of goose" in England, and similar in form to games of the snakes-and-ladders type.

Minotaur, as well as the age of onset of adolescence in Greece). One square was called the *Minesthaurus.* The game told the story of a "voyage of the hunted," in which chance determined the moves (see illustration #53).

Some of these games recount the story of the Hundred Years War; still others, the conflict between the Jesuits and the Jansenists. Then a version became a device for lovers' declarations in France, when the *Précieux* movement produced the *Carte du Tendre,* a kind of labyrinthic board game for lovers, in the form of a map. Louis XIII was a fanatic player of this game; and Saint-Simon wrote that "the Dauphiness, shut up in her apartments, turns to the goose game for consolation." According to Arnaud, Napoleon "plunged into this game with a truly Mediterranean passion, counting the squares with his middle finger like a schoolboy, becoming surly when the dice went against him, always going moodily into the 'cabaret,' cheating for fear of falling into the 'well,' or going to 'prison,' facing 'death' with anxiety, and displaying the whole contrasting range of his personality through the vicissitudes of this contest."[122]

New games such as Monopoly, Chutes and Ladders, Sorry, and Trivial Pursuit appeared in the twentieth century, all maintaining the goal of traversing a winding path strewn with obstacles or trials.

In card games, the archetype of success is surely that of solitary passage through a labyrinth. Most often, one wants to achieve the longest possible path without going backwards and without coming back to the starting point. A dead end is a false victory, a premature arrival. Among card games played with partners, which involve battles of one sort or another, death waits in ambush in the concealed hand of the adversary, a labyrinth that one attempts to discover and penetrate. Both good and bad luck lie in wait, hidden in the deal or in the discards.

Though belonging to a very different category, the game of billiards is also labyrinthic, a labyrinth of points and black holes wound in exotic circles determined by more or less direct contact between orbs set in motion by a cue (gravity). But the loftiest of all of such games is chess. Here, one must pass through a labyrinth that is constantly reinvented by the adversary, threading one's way towards the opposing King, and at the same time constructing a labyrinth to protect one's own King. It is a thoroughly nomadic game, easily carried along in one's travels. It is a game of initiates par excellence (memorizing openings, remembering classic plays, and having tenacity), and a gentlemanly contest among adepts—generally, the loser resigns, the winner never actually administering the fatal blow to the King, and most games are abandoned much earlier, sometimes even many moves in advance of the inevitable end. Chess was probably one of the very first surrogates for war, and the first "virtualization" of war, with its labyrinthine strategies.

Finally, we come to puzzles, which reproduce a labyrinthine design, and demand similar qualities of methodical patience, perseverance, and systematic thinking, as does the labyrinth.

And we must not neglect to mention those ancestral games of knots, where one must weave an interlacing pattern out of a single string, tied with artistic simplicity.[30]

Sports: from Speed to Labyrinth

All these games have been overshadowed by rectilinear sports, in which the aim is simply to go or to throw further, higher, and faster. The Olympic movement as a whole has been founded upon a defense of rectitude, transparence, and speed as the primary values of success. Such sports require neither ruse nor any of the other qualities typical of the labyrinth. They are races, distance heaves, and shots at targets. On the other hand, it would seem that in game-based sports we leave rectilinearity, since playing a game always comes back, in some degree, to striving to overcome or get around an obstacle, or to resolve a puzzle.

Labyrinthic sports have long existed—all sorts of ball games involving teams, such as soccer, rugby, football, hockey, and lacrosse aim to get through the adversarial labyrinth by setting up one's own impenetrable labyrinth of obstacles as one

advances, much as in chess. Basketball was proposed as a rectilinear competition by its inventor James Naismith, the dribbles
meant merely to slow progress; yet it was turned labyrinthine by
folk athletes, as the dribbles become a dance of twisting pathways and routes toward and away from the center, the net.
Baseball is a different kind of labyrinth, with its pre-Copernican
epicycles and translations of force and strength into obstacles as
well as achievements. Slowness, change of tempo, and place-
ment (as in a bunt) are as crucial as great speed or distance and
wind the players in a labyrinth of plays and statistics. Golf (links)
is another obstacle-strewn course with numerous impasses and
traps. Originally it was played in Scottish and Dutch villages,
with obstacles formed by houses, the town green, and even
plowed fields.

Some "rectilinear" sports can become complex and mazelike
at times, such as running hurdles, rafting, automobile rallies, and
so on, always in contrast to a simple speed course.

I would not hesitate to wager that labyrinthine games will
conquer all the others before too long. After all, the purpose of
games has always been to imitate real life, and hence to prepare
players for it.

Playing in a Maze

New labyrinthic games are now being concocted in a playful
kind of landscape. The first to appear were video games, which
involve passing through trials and obstacles. The major success
of this exploding market include Doom, Mario Brothers, Street
Fighter, Alone in the Dark, and Virtual Fighter. But the CD-ROM
itself is structured exactly like a labyrinth, and teaches one to
"think the labyrinth." Beyond this, there is the Internet, which
would seem to be the children's playground of the future, a place
where they will lose themselves, find themselves, and invent
games of the most varied forms. Children of modern societies
will search out the means to defy labyrinths, to bring their secrets
to light. They will play an *active* role in these games, for when
they reach adulthood their very life will depend on being active
in labyrinths.

Everything will become a labyrinthic game. Healing and therapeutic care will be done through games; witness homeopathy, reflexology, and diagnosis by visceral manipulation. Education is already using CD-ROMS as devices of initiation into play-oriented education, which has been called "edutainment."

Games are the enemy of wars, since they replace them by simulations. They embody courtesy and consideration, because they presuppose agreement on rules. The most playful peoples are the least warlike and the most civilized. Tomorrow's video games will be even more explicit in providing a competitive alternative to what we experience today as war, violence, and terrorism.

But play is not just distraction. In the labyrinths of tomorrow, play will become an ethic of life, a way of being free. And learning how to reflect, to challenge, and to trick is also a way of enjoyment that goes beyond money.

Tricking

How to Find the Way

There is no a priori requirement of any sort of intelligence in order to go through a labyrinth. One simply advances. If it has dead ends, one needs luck, memory, and perseverance. But there is no prior formula for a rational choice between one path over another. The interlocking pattern of its forks and impasses obeys no law but the imagination of its designer.

Everything depends upon what one is able to surmise about its structure—are its walls smooth and unbroken? Might there not be some sign, even an unintentional one, lying on the ground? Is there a significance to the pattern of its turns? Is the best choice more often to the left than to the right?

In order to answer such questions, we must try to proceed with a systematic exploration of all possible choices, just as one works out algorithms to evaluate all the hypotheses involved before making a decision. But more often than not, such an exercise is in vain. It is better to use one's intelligence to guess the right road. But what sort of intelligence? Reason will not get us far, for the labyrinth is not at all rational. We must see, feel, and sense our way.

And we must listen. Is not the ear itself a labyrinth, a spiral of two and a half octaves, yet able to hear far more than these? Are not the two extreme notes of a musical scale like two neighboring points in a labyrinth, so close, yet so far from each other?

Cunning

Yet more still is required of us: all our senses must be on the alert, so that we can learn to navigate both with a sense of the immediate, and an eye fixed on the long term. This type of intelligence reaches beyond reason, to the intuition of the mariner, the hunter, the nomad. We call it cunning, or *ruse*.

The Greeks long ago defined this type of intelligence, which they contrasted with reason, as *metis,* from the name of Zeus's first wife, the mother of Athena, whom the god devoured so as to assimilate her powers, which would enable him to forestall the other gods' ruses.

From Sailor to Diplomat

Ruse is the principal quality of navigators: it helps the steersman to follow the coastline, even when tacking against the wind, guiding the vessel to its destination by a route best adapted to unstable and unpredictable elements. Sophocles placed navigation in the highest rank of human skills, possessed by those who are considered to be "resourceful," the decipherers of roads, or *pantaporos."* To find a path, a *poros,* an opening or an expedient, to work cunningly with the wind, to be forever on the alert, to foresee the most propitious moment for action—all these activities, all these skills, demand a multi-faceted intelligence."[36] Ulysses, the "man of a thousand ruses...who knows all sorts of tricks...who knows how to weave plots," is the prototype of the navigator. Pindar called him the "protean trickster," this man who set a trap for his rivals—a trap that happened to be a net, another allusion to the motion of fish in the nets, one of the images of the labyrinth.

Cunning is also necessary in commerce, which is structured not by reason but by ruse. In order to negotiate a contract or a sale, one must know how to feel one's way, estimating with rough guesses, not being swayed by logical arguments, advancing and yielding, giving and taking, circling around one's goal without making it obvious.

Cunning is also the major talent of the diplomat, who must imagine somewhat in advance the movements of volatile coalitions, with hunches of what will transpire, inviting, seducing, flattering, compromising, laying traps, sensing what the others want, convincing them to accept as a victory what is actually a compromise.

Cunning is also one of the greatest qualities of a physician. Arriving at a diagnosis is exactly like threading a labyrinth; a good doctor must employ this type of mobile, intuitive intelligence in order to plumb the unknown, exploring diverse paths and recognizing dead ends before arriving at the result.

And there is no politics without cunning. Aristotle already explained the indispensability of *metis* in politics, "where success depends more on an appraising glance than on enduring knowledge."[36]

War without cunning does not exist. Here too, superior force is not the primary source of victory. One must know how to wait at the right place for the right moment. This is the aim of guerrilla action, and this principle will also characterize the few nation-states that survive the times to come.

Intelligent Spying

Cunning will also be the main quality needed for economic progress. Just as a nomadic economy's primary wealth resides in strategic knowledge, so in interconnected technological labyrinths, those who know the networks will control the primary source of increased profits. The acquisition of such knowledge implies considerable cunning. First of all, the creation of these labyrinths in research and development labs will require a non-rational intelligence; and then cunning will be needed by those who wrest access to them from their authors or proprietors. It will also be needed to discover their routes and patterns, and to protect oneself from others' trickery, thanks to a planetary "intelligence" network—one that is used both by researchers and by spies—to find out what is being developed elsewhere, and also to protect one's own discoveries from theft attempts. Its users will learn both to fasten and to unravel the knots of new knowledge.

Unraveling

The orienting thread that enables us to backtrack to where we have been defines at once the longest and the most direct path out of the labyrinth. This is the path that extracts us from our snarls and solves the puzzle.

Tying Knots

In the art of tying and untying knots, one finds the best approximation of the qualities needed for traveling through labyrinths. A kind of labyrinth itself, the knot is composed of twists, loops, and braids, and is also a place of convergence of all sorts of energies. Like the labyrinth, it conceals an enigma: one speaks of the "untangling" of a plot, and the "knot" of a problem.

In many civilizations, knot and labyrinth are both metaphors for destiny. Like the labyrinth, the knot is related to death—sometimes as announcer of it, sometimes as protection from it.

For some peoples, bearing a knot on one's person brings bad luck by attracting and trapping evil.[28] In India, knots are also associated with death. Both in Iran and among Australian aborigines one can kill at a distance merely by tying a knot while thinking of the victim. In Greece, the Fates determined destiny and fixed the hour of death by means of knotted cords.

Talismans

In other places, on the contrary (but for the same reason of trapping evil), the knot is a talisman of protection. It has a magical relation to death, as in Arabia, where a sorcerer foils a curse by knotting stems of wheat. Pilgrims en route to Mecca must have knots in their clothes, but they must untie them when arriving before the Kaaba. In Morocco, families treat their sick by hanging knots from trees. This recalls practices in China and in India, where a labyrinth is drawn on the roof of a house in order to frustrate evil spirits, which always travel in a straight line.[28]

Often, being cured is equated with untying a knot. In the Upanishads, "to untangle the knot of the heart" signifies "to attain immortality." Yet the knot also unites mankind to God, Brahmins to Brahman, and is a symbol of longevity. The same idea recurs in the Kabbalistic tradition; according to Abraham Abulafia, the goal of life is to "unseal the soul," to "unfasten the bonds" which confine it. Only when this is done can one begin the "true life" of a human being freed from earthly bonds.

In other cases, the knot grants life, as among the Bambaras, whose god Amsa sends them a covenant ark suspended by a cord.[28] In Egypt, a special knot ties together the parts of the body of Osiris which were cut into pieces by Seth, thus empowering his resurrection.[30]

Textile and Text

In a great many cultures, the knot, like the labyrinth, is considered to be the primordial structure of language. The Dogon of Africa say that three languages appeared in succession: braiding, weaving, and the game of threads.[30] The first language was revealed through the fashioning of the skirt of Mother Earth by two twins, using fibers taken from plants previously created in the Sky. Their spindle was a channel for the words of the gods. The second language was revealed through the weaving of the words of the first. The third came through the game of threads, or "cat's nests." In many other cultures, including the Incas, but especially among maritime peoples, the knot is employed as a means of writing.

Woven fabric is often designated by a name that also means text, as in the title of this section. The Internet itself is a kind of fabric woven from texts.

Weaving appears at exactly the same Neolithic stage as labyrinths, from Peru to the Near East. While Ulysses threads the oceanic labyrinth, Penelope weaves; and it is a thread that Ariadne gives to Theseus. In numerous cultures, woven cloth is decorated with designs of labyrinths, including the San Blas islanders off the Panamanian coast, the Yorubas of Nigeria, the Fons of Benin, The Foutis of Ghana, and the Kubas of Zaïre (see illustrations #71 through #74).[14]

The tying and untying of knots is primarily a feminine occupation. But the weaving of cloth is not the only path which leads to wisdom—our planet is now in the process of being clothed in a threadless fabric whose loom is composed of countless millions of computers linked together. Whoever wishes to design their own labyrinthine architectures within it would do well to know the laws and tricks of weaving. A major form of expertise will be based on the knowledge of how to entangle and disentangle such networks, creating added value and profits. Software will take on an aspect of a game of threads. This science will also serve as a tool for unraveling terrorist networks.

The knot brings us to our final quality necessary for threading labyrinths: painstaking thoroughness, which enables us to act without losing patience, with a systematic thinking that respects the order of facts and deeds.

Learning to disentangle complex knots is a philosophical apprenticeship of great use for the mastery of the future. It requires calm, equanimity, perseverance, detachment, and an acuity of regard, all of which are necessary abilities for anticipating the labyrinths to come. Surely these could be cultivated in schools, along with a process of learning how to elucidate ever more complex enigmas.

Elucidating

This is the culminating phase for those who have been able to cultivate all of the necessary qualities of this course. Those who approach the exit may rightly fear that the freedom in sight could be no more than a mirage, for they do not know whether this opening is really an exit or a return to the entrance. But they understand that getting all the way through is possible, for a labyrinth can by definition be solved.

Getting Out of a Design

But what does this mean in practice? Are there solutions which can be employed in any labyrinth?

Not quite. A labyrinth drawn on paper can be solved by shading in all the dead ends progressively, so that only the correct path is what finally remains. Or, one can sometimes shorten the solution time by working backwards from the goal.

Passing Through Corridors

On the other hand, as Greg Bright suggests, a paper labyrinth may also be explored by cutting a hole in a blank piece of paper, and sliding this "eye" along the corridors of the labyrinth, thus simulating the experience of someone inside a real labyrinth.[17] For the latter, there are some traditional methods (which can be used in video games as well as in park or garden labyrinths), but none are infallible. The first consists of advancing while keeping one hand in contact with the wall. This can work, except when there are two entrances connected by a path which does not go to the goal, or when there is a path which goes in a circle around the goal (a device that labyrinth designers typically favor).[87]

The French mathematician Trémieux offers another, virtually universal, approach to solving mazes: he advises treaders to keep touching the right-hand wall while advancing. If they reach a dead end, they must double back by the same path, still touching the same wall, until they reach a fork previously encountered; here, they must take a new path (if there is one), or a path that has not previously been walked in both directions. Of course this method does not guarantee success in every case, nor does it necessarily find the best possible path.[114]

To think like a nomad, to face up, to get lost, to accept oneself, to persevere, to remember, to dance, to play, to trick, to elucidate: whoever is able to unite all these qualities has every chance of progressing, even after countless mistakes, towards the answer to the only question that matters: *What do I want to become?*

Labyrinthing

What is it that one feels upon emerging from a labyrinth? Deliverance? An impression of completion? Or, on the contrary, a feeling of loss, lack, or light-headedness? "The labyrinth is not a place where one gets lost—it is after leaving it that one always feels lost," wrote Michel Foucault.

However that may be, travelling through a labyrinth—even if it happens only once—transforms consciousness forever. Having experienced being lost means having opened all the doors of oneself, and exploring oneself. As a "hunted voyager," one has not found the truth, but a road towards a more difficult question.[40] The one who has "encountered the reality of experience," as Joyce says, is also, in the words of Nietzsche, "the labyrinthine man who never seeks the truth, but always and only his Ariadne."[95]

Such is the great secret of the labyrinth, which enables those who confront it to be healed.

Healing

The First Sorcerers

The most ancient wisdom traditions teach that one can find healing by going through a labyrinth. They found that even the simple mental exercise of traversing a labyrinth with the eyes could engender an inner voyage, bringing calm and serenity. With this knowledge, ancient peoples developed different forms of these healing lab yrinths, adapted to different afflictions of body and mind.

At the temple of Thalos in Epidauros, near the shrine of Aesculapius, patients followed the course of a labyrinth to free them of their illnesses.[113] This was also the hope of many pilgrims who walked church labyrinths. Among the Navajos today, there are labyrinthine designs intended to lead the sick person back to the origin of the world, whereupon the medicine-man identifies the disease and the imbalance which is its cause.[132] He then performs chants and dances corresponding to its nature. A labyrinthine sand-painting is constructed with raw materials, symbols, and shapes corresponding to the journey of the illness. The ceremony may last two, three, five, or nine days, depending on the gravity of the situation. On the final day, the medicine-man pours out sand of different colors, made with dyes from charcoal, flowers, or corn, onto the naked body of the patient. This both purifies the person and enables him to trap the malevolent entities in the sand-painted labyrinth. Finally, the painting is dispersed—the most delicate part of the operation—which brings the healing.

The Zulus tattoo themselves with spiral and labyrinthine designs to protect their souls from a goddess who is said to blind anyone who lacks such tattoos. Cuna women protect themselves from illness with labyrinths. The Nazcas pass through a labyrinth depicting a certain animal, so as to absorb its strength. The Chinese perform "labyrinth dances" in order to heal various illnesses, and draw labyrinths at the entrances of houses as protection from evil spirits. In southern India, women paint labyrinths on the floor of their dwellings at dawn during the season of danger, and men must traverse them. A labyrinth (the *Chakra Vyuha*) served in the *Mahabharata* to help a woman give birth, showing her the way through a difficult labor. In Tibet, the mandala serves as an aid to meditation, a representation of the path to Divinity, as well as a protection device, and a tool for concentration.[22] Its central point, the *bindu,* which is the meditator's focus, unites energies. Through mandala meditation, the sick person travels from outside to inside oneself, attaining fulfillment. Contemplating the *bindu* brings security through a return to the natural order and to physical and mental wholeness; such practice is a condition for maintaining health.[122]

Veriditas

The healing labyrinth has returned to the modern and, like so many other formerly esoteric and hermetic disciplines and rituals, has been revived in a public, democratic, and exoteric context. In a time of history when one can enroll in a shamanic vision quest, sand-painting ritual, or ancient Tibetan visualization ritual with the ease of signing up for white-water rafting or tango lessons, one can also "walk a labyrinth" at a number of churches, hospitals, and spiritual centers worldwide. Some of these labyrinths are built in place; others, printed on mats or fabrics, can be transported from site to site or put down at different times. In the United States alone, there are hundreds of healing labyrinths, including at the Meridian Church of the Mediator in Mississippi; the Haden Institute in Charlotte, North Carolina; the Louisiana State Medical Center in New Orleans; Harmony Hill Retreat and Healing Center on Hood Canal in the State of Washington; Unity Churches throughout the country (for instance, in Denver); Northwoods Presbyterian Church in Houston, Texas; East Liberty Presbyterian Church in Pittsburgh, Pennsylvania; Culver Palms United Methodist Church in Culver City, California; and Hennepin Avenue United Methodist Church in Minneapolis, Minnesota. One Web site lists more than a hundred labyrinths in the United States, but there are undoubtedly many more. In San Diego, there is a woman who carries a cloth labyrinth to her local jails for prisoners to walk. In California, students at several universities walk them before exams. The California Pacific Medical Center in San Francisco, an acute-care hospital, has a painted labyrinth outside the entrance that is walked by emergency-room nurses as well as patients and their families—and at least three more hospitals across the country are planning labyrinths of their own. The St. Louis Labyrinth Project in Missouri uses a 100-foot diameter replica of the Chartres eleven-circuit pattern, which is walked by visitors for global and personal peace.

Rev. Dr. Lauren Artress is a psychotherapist with a divinity degree who became convinced of the power of labyrinths in

1991. "When you walk into the labyrinth," she told an interviewer, "the mind quiets, and then you begin to see through what's happening inside. You become transparent to yourself. You can see that you're scared, or frightened, or that you lack courage. People can see for the first time that their anger is in the way. You can see your judgments against people and against yourself." Soon after her first labyrinth walk, Rev. Artress traveled to see the Chartres labyrinth in France, which had fallen completely out of practical use. She measured its dimensions with the goal of duplicating it in the Grace Cathedral in San Francisco. Grace Cathedral now has two such labyrinths, one an outdoor stone terrazzo grid, the other a Chartres-type grid. Artress' worldwide labyrinth project called Veriditas has since distributed thousands of kits on how to design a labyrinth. She has trained hundreds of people, via workshops, in how to organize labyrinth walks. At her Grace Cathedral walks, where sometimes Taizé music is played, a wide range of participants come with different agendas: a couple walks it every year on their anniversary, a pregnant woman has found that walking it quiets her kicking baby, and a group of women undergoing chemotherapy walk it together. People walking labyrinths report, variously, a spontaneous transformation of consciousness, an experience of the feminine aspects of the divine, an increasing depth of walking meditation (as occurs while walking in between sessions of zazen), a sense of the hidden numbers joining spirit and matter, a vision of a spider's web from within, a dance of atoms, a joining of the two halves of the brain, and a feeling of the planets and moons in orbit. Some report an interesting distortion of time and space such that other people walking the labyrinth at the same time approach and drift apart. Some people close by are actually quite faraway in the meandering of the pattern and other people who seem on the far side of the design are only a minute or two ahead. Rev. Artress' next project is the reopening of the Chartres Cathedral; the rector there visited the Grace Cathedral and witnessed the revival of the labyrinth ritual.

So does the death, rebirth, and migration of the labyrinth also prescribe a labyrinthic rune on space and time. Artress proposes that rather than partying on New Year's Eve 2000, people should gather in labyrinths all over the world. The symbolic gateway to the millennium would then recall the original passage through tribal mythology into history.

For those who wish to explore further, prominent labyrinth Web sites include:

http://www.gracecom.org/veriditas /

www.azlink.com/~labyrinth/tr/

www.1.heart.com/labyrinth.html

www.ashlandweb.com/humdev/laby.html

www.geomancy.org/labyrint/labyrint.html

Videotherapy

Today, specific video games are used to help sick children take charge of their illness by "playing" themselves in a combat against their virus. This is a kind of therapeutic self-apprentice-ship. Virtual images of labyrinths are used as simulations of dangerous situations. One can thus heal oneself of vertigo or acrophobia (the complex of Icarus) in passing through labyrinths of virtual threats.

The labyrinth will always be a kind of breach between two worlds (as Castaneda says of the twilight), and a prison for evil. It is also a consolation, helping to cure the ravages of jealousy, desire, pride, hatred, stupidity, and rivalry.

All of us must learn to play its instruments, to create our own mental labyrinths, using our vision to follow labyrinthine paths in a kind of daily aerobics of the mind. Finally, we must each learn to invent our own labyrinths—the art of "labyrinthing."

Labyrinthing

How to Create a Labyrinth

The ultimate exercise of freedom is the creation of labyrinths. This may be a mere exercise or an illusion, but it is also a game involving the highest stakes of technology and politics. For each of us will have need of this knowledge in order to succeed in all facets of human activity.

One may exercise this by drawing blindly, by following artistic intuition, by obeying technical rules, or by applying ancient principles. In order to create a labyrinth which is both complex and esthetically satisfying, the ancient wisdom traditions recommend beginning by defining the area to be filled in, outlining it with some kind of shape, selecting a unified style of paths (straight and/or curved), choosing a goal (a center to be found, a space to be travelled through), and one or more entrances.[114] At this point, one may trace out the path which leads to the goal, followed by the dead ends. One must avoid overly long straight-aways, and dead ends that are too obvious or too much alike. And there are certain tricks of the trade; for example, using the fact that most labyrinth travelers tend to turn more often right than left, one puts most dead ends to the right, and the correct path to the left. Finally, one must remember to fill the space in a uniform manner, with paths of equal width, and never leaving empty or forgotten spaces in the area.

The drawing of a circular labyrinth is especially simple, and worth an effort by anyone who gets all the way through this book. Here is an elementary labyrinthing exercise: first, draw concentric circles; then place bars and erase small segments of the circles to make openings, thereby creating paths (see illustration #82). Another very ancient method for drawing a labyrinth of three circuits consists of drawing a cross and placing one dot in each quadrant. Then one draws a small clockwise semicircle, joining the top endpoint of the cross to the dot placed in the upper right quadrant; this is followed by a semicircle joining the dot in the upper left quadrant to the endpoint of the cross's right arm, and then the endpoint of the cross's left arm to the next dot in the lower right quadrant—a natural and intuitive process that results in a three-circuit labyrinth found in ancient cultures in Crete, Sweden, and Arizona. In order to construct the famous seven-circuit Cretan labyrinth, one starts with a cross outlined by "L" shapes, with dots placed in the outer quadrants formed by the L's (see illustration #79), proceeding in the same logical and intuitive manner. A double-L shape at the beginning suffices to create an eleven-circuit labyrinth of this type.[87]

A labyrinth designer is a transformer of the finite into the quasi-infinite, coiling time up into a limited space, just as humans pack time into their artifacts. The artisan transmutes the simple into the complex, giving life, and thus becoming godlike. Daedalus gave life to statues and animated a cow. In his labyrinths, Da Vinci mingled cords and branches, artifacts, and nature.[18] The creation of labyrinths thereby becomes an art that is both ironic and sacred. From Daedalus to Ecarlate, down to the architects of software and computer networks—these are the masters of such voyages throughout the centuries. In the future, as in the ancient past, labyrinth creators will produce beautiful and difficult things. The esthetic of the labyrinth resides in its difficulty: *Per ardua ad astra.*

Is the labyrinth the beginning of art? A masking, a tricking, a decoy-filled camouflaging of the path, a work of art is a trap. The first prehistoric gestures which one could call artistic — whether among aborigines, Africans, Indians, or Celts—were all inspired by labyrinths. One of the most explicit is the art of the Australians, much of which consisted of labyrinths "to guide future initiates in their mental processes."[8] In Crete, seal engravers avoided symmetry in their art, making each seal a unique and identifying emblem.

More generally, every artistic creation is labyrinthine in nature: the solitude and doubts of the creator are of exactly the same order as the experience of going through the labyrinth, not knowing in advance whether an exit or solution will be found. The work of art is the result of a labyrinthine journey. Even the path followed by the gaze of the spectator of a painting resembles a labyrinthine path. Once the eye has "swept" the picture in this way, it can be recollected as a whole. Thus Jorge Luis Borges defined the esthetic act as "the imminence of a revelation which does not come to pass."[15] Again, this is exactly the experience of the labyrinth voyager.

This is also exactly what is needed in order to elucidate all sorts of other problems—seeking out information in the meanders of the brain, creating improbable connections between different zones of the cortex—this is what helps very young children succeed, for it is the key to the process of creation.

Faced with a blank sheet of paper, the first creative tracings of a young child are typically some sort of labyrinth. And the most elite practitioners of the future, whether painters, urbanists, choreographers, or network architects, will continue to reproduce such tracings.

Art and the Mask

Every society appraises and judges itself by the artistic traces it leaves. A nineteenth-century vicar in the Cotswolds in England trained a ridge structure into a maze to illustrate the concepts of *Pilgrim's Progress*. Contemporary art is returning to the labyrinth, to "portable frescos," as Jackson Pollock's work has been described. The labyrinth is one of the themes of Escher's work (see illustration #76), and in surrealist paintings—those of Delvaux, for example—the points furthest from each other are in reality the nearest, separated by a purely conventional obstacle. The labyrinthine designs on cloth by such peoples as the Kubas of Zaïre (see illustrations #71 and #74), and especially by the Shuras, inspired the designs of Kandinsky, Dubuffet, Klee, and Sonia Delaunay. Paul Klee gave a most precise description of the labyrinthine nature of primitive art: "What existed in the beginning? Things moved, so to speak, in complete freedom, neither in a straight line nor in a curved line. They must be thought of as fundamentally mobile, going wherever they go, wandering without goal, without will, without obedience, an expression of the natural obviousness of moving, the state of original motion."[8]

Francis Bacon wrote, in the same vein, "I would like for my paintings to give the impression that a man has left his tracks there like a snail, leaving a trail of human presence and the memory of past events just as a snail leaves its trail of saliva."

The same is true of music. In its long meanderings, it has served as a means of taming time, in the art of improvisation; or of roaming freely on the basis of a given theme, a practice which culminates in Bach, the last representative of the most extreme form of musical labyrinth, the fugue. The standardized architecture of harmony dominated for almost two centuries afterward. Then came a return of the labyrinth at the beginning of our era, with music drawing inspiration from primitivism, as with Debussy or Ravel's *Bolero*. Luciano Berio wrote that "The labyrinth is an open form which allows several interpretations, as in jazz improvisations."[107] Music is developing more and more in this way, and this applies to "popular" music, "serious" music, and other forms—all of them composed of blind alleys and repeats.

Such will be the nature of the art and the esthetics of tomorrow.

The nomad creators of the labyrinths of the future will win the right to wear their own masks; from child to mother, from earthly to celestial, they will be able to thread the path, accept fear, untie knots, and open the gates of Heaven. Like the young Hopis, they will discover that the *kachinas,* the dolls with which they play, are the spirits which are their closest kin. They will not leave the world; they will grow, having learned that the essence of life is found in movement, in the quest.

If it is for us that our remotest Ancestors have left all those tracings on walls, like prisoners leaving graffiti in their cells, then it is because they are crying out for us to not forget the ancient wisdom, holding messages for the survival of the human species: to discover who one is, to learn to experience time like space, to draw strength from error, to trace out one's life like a labyrinth, never ceasing to improvise. This is to make life into a game and a work of art, "to enchant oneself," as Plato put it, to seek out the roads of one's own serene perfection, with a distant irony, in remembrance of the nomad's knowledge, in the pleasure of being stopped or led astray—if only in order to prepare oneself for the ultimate, inevitable sedentary voyage that awaits everyone.

The nomad is the creator of God, and has need of Him as a restorative, as the hope towards which one's regard is always turned, a guide and consoler.

In the labyrinths of the deserts of tomorrow, solitude will recreate this need for solidarity, mutual assistance, belonging, and spirituality, this need for a portable God or its technological simulacrum. However that may be, the nomads of tomorrow will once again have need of a Sacrament that can be carried in a backpack, a mobile God. After the Walkman will come the Walkgod, a portable link with the beyond.

In this sense, the third millennium will be mystical, because it will be nomadic. In solitude, every individual will become like a thread of a fabric, a word of a text, a cell of a living organism, a point in an enveloping and transcending labyrinth. Each individual will be a particle of the God which one carries along.

It is quite probable that this same millennium will also see eruptions here and there of extreme totalitarianism, obtuse sectarianism, and terrifying violence. But those who understand how the labyrinths of tomorrow fit into a historical and mythological continuity will be able to fulfill their roles as inheritors of these very ancient vicissitudes. They will realize that the most futuristic economics, the most leading-edge science-fiction, the most outlandish geopolitical theories, all take their place as new avatars of a very ancient tradition, among the threads woven by the loom of human history.

It is forgetfulness that could kill humanity. The memory of what we have read in the tracks of our nomadic predecessors will save us, opening up the way towards a civilized use of our creations, an economy based on pleasure, freedom, and humor.

Courage will be needed, for *at the exit of every kind of labyrinth, humankind will never find anything but other labyrinths*. Labyrinths of labyrinths. Some will believe they are meeting God; others, the truth; and others will experience an ironic skepticism or a despairing panic. And finally, still others will find an enigmatic and fragile path towards Wisdom.

Bibliography

1. Antier, Gilles, "Pékin et Shanghai," *Hérodote,* no. 49.

2. Attali, Jacques, *L'Ordre cannibale,* Grasset, Paris, 1979.

3. Attali, Jacques, *Lignes d'horizon,* Fayard, 1989.

4. Attali, Jacques, *Histoires du temps,* Fayard, Paris, 1982.

5. Audouze, Jean; Cassé, Michel; Carrière, Jean-Claude, *Conversations sur l'invisible,* Plon, Paris, 1996.

6. Balandier, Georges, *Le Dédale. Pour en finir avec le XXe siècle,* Fayard, 1994.

7. Barral I. Altet, Xavier, *Compostelle. Le grand chemin,* Découvertes Gallimard, 1993.

8. Barou, Jean-Pierre, *L'Oeil pense,* Ballard, 1993.

9. Bayard, Jean-Pierre, *La Tradition cachée des cathédrales,* Dangles, 1990.

10. Bayard, Jean-Pierre, *Le Monde souterrain,* Flammarion, 1961.

11. Bofill, Ricardo; Veron, Nicolas, *L'Architecture des villes,* Odile Jacob, 1995.

12. Boitard, Roger, *L'Art de composer les jardins,* Beaubourg.

13. Bonnet, Roger M., *Horizons chimériques,* Dunod, Paris, 1992.

14. Bord, Janet; Lambert, J.-C., *Labyrinthes et dédales du monde,* Paris, Presses de la Connaissance, 1977.

15. Borges, Jorge Luis, *L'Aleph,* "L'Imaginaire," Gallimard, 1977.

16. Bourdarias, Jean, *Guide européen des chemins de Compostelle,* Fayard, 1996.

17. Bright, Greg, *The Great Maze Book,* Presses de la Connaissance.

18. Brion, Marcel, *L'Art fantastique,* Albin Michel, 1989.

19. Buber, Martin, *The Way of Man: According to the Teaching of Hasidism,* Le Rocher, 1989.

20. Bulletin consacré au Tumulus de Gavrinis, *Association archéologique Kergal,* mai 1977.

21. Caillois, Roger, *Les Jeux et les sports,* Gallimard, Bibliothèque de la Pléiade, 1968.

22. Caillois, Roger, *Les Jeux et les hommes,* Gallimard, 1967.

23. Campbell, Joseph, *The Masks of God,* vol. I: *Primitive Mythology* (New York, 1959) — *Les Héros sont éternels,* Seghers, 1987.

24. Canteins, Jean, *Dédale et ses oeuvres, le potier démiurge,* Maisonneuve et Larose, 1986.

25. Caruana, Wally, *Aboriginal Art (The World of Art),* Thames & Hudson, Paris, 1994.

26. Champion, Alex, *Earth Mazes,* Albany, California, 1990.

27. Chaucer, Geoffrey, *The Canterbury Tales,* Peeters, 1983, 1996.

28. Chevalier, Jean; Gheerbrant, Alain, *A Dictionary of Symbols,* Robert Laffont, 1970.

29. Comte-Sponville, André, *The Myth of Icarus,* PUF, 1984.

30. Conti Patrick, *The Geometry of the Labyrinth,* Albin Michel, 1996.

31. Cook, Thomas Genn, *Koster. An Artifactual Analysis of Tow Archaic Phases in Western Illinois,* Evanston, Ill., 1976.

32. Dejean René, *Les Traboules de Lyon. Histoire secrète d'une ville.*

33. Deeds, C.N., *Labyrinths and Mazes.*

34. Delft, Pieter Van; Botermans, Jack, *Mille cassetête du monde entier,* Le Chêne, 1987.

35. Descartes, René, *Discourse on Method,* Corpus de philosophie en langue française, Fayard, 1987.

36. Detienne, Marcel; Vernant, Jean-Pierre, *Les Ruses de l'intelligence, la Mètis des Grecs,* "Champs," Flammarion, Paris, 1989.

37. Diel, Paul, *Symbolism in Greek Mythology: Human Desire and its Transformations,* Payot, 1966, 1989.

38. Diodore de Sicile, *Bibliothèque historique,* Belles lettres.

39. Eco, Umberto, *The Name of the Rose,* Poche/Essais, 1987.

40. Eliade, Mircea, *L'Épreuve de labyrinthe,* Belfond, 1978, 1985.

41. Eliade, Mircea, *Myth of the Eternal Return,* Gallimard, 1969, 1989.

42. Eliot, Alexander; Campbell, Jeseph; Eliade, Mircea, *The Universal Myths: Heroes, Gods, Tricksters and Others,* Éd. Sous-le-Vent, 1976.

43. Elkin A.P., *The Austrailian Aborigines,* Gallimard, 1968.

44. *World Mythology,* Larousse, 1935, 1992.

45. Faure, Élie, *L'Esprit des formes,* Paris, 1964, 1989.

46. Faure, Paul, *La Vie quotidienne en Crète au temps de Minos,* hachette, 1973.

47. Faure, Paul, *Ulysse le Crétois,* Fayard, 1980.

48. Fischer, Adrian; Gester, George, *The Art of the Maze,* Londres, 1990.

49. Fischer, Adrian, *The Art of the Maze.*

50. Focillon, Henri, *Le Moyen Age roman. Le Moyen Age gothique,* Livre de Poche, 1988.

51. Fondation Dapper, *Abstraction au royaume des kuba,* 1990.

52. Fondation Dapper, *Au royaume des signes,* 1992.

53. Forest, Philippe, *Textes et labyrinthes.*

54. Fraser, J.T., *Time,* British Library.

55. Freud, Sigmund, *Oeuvres,* PUF.

56. Frontisi-Ducroux, Françoise, *Dédale: Mythologie de l'artisan en Grèce ancienne,* Découverte, Paris, 1975.

57. Fulcanelli, *Mystery of the Cathédrals,* Pauvert, 1965, 1983.

58. Gaudin, Henri, *La Cabane et le labyrinthe,* Mardaga, 1973, 1984.

59. Gide, Andre, *Thésée,* Gallimard Folio, 1981.

60. Graves, Robert, *The Greek Myths,* Fayard, 1967.

61. Graves, Robert, *La Toison d'or,* Gallimard, 1964; *The Hebrew Myths,* Fayard, 1987; *The White Goddess,* Le Rocher, 1979.

62. Graves, Tom, *The Diviner's Handbook,* Thorsons/The Aquarian Press, 1986; *Needles of Stone Revisited,* Gothic Image, 1986.

63. Griaule, Marcel, *Dieu d'eau,* Fayard, 1966.

64. Grimal, Pierre, *Dictionary of Greek and Roman Mythology,* PUF, 1951, 1990.

65. Guénon, Robert, *Les Symboles fondamentaux de la science sacrée,* Gallimard, 1962.

66. Hérodote, *Histoires,* Belles lettres.

67. Hocke, G.R., *Labyrinthe de l'art fantastique,* Gonthier/Denoël, 1967, 1977.

68. Hofstadter, Douglas, *Gödel, Escher, Bach: les brins d'une guirlande éternelle,* Interéditions, 1985.

69. Homer, *Iliad* and *Odyssey,* La Pléiade, Gallimard, 1955.

70. Jabès, Edmond, *The Book of Questions,* "L'Imaginaire," Gallimard, 1963.

71. Jacquard, Albert; Lacarrière, Jacques, *Sciences et croyances,* Ecriture, Paris, 1994.

72. James, John, *The Master-Builders of Chartres,* J.-M. Garnier, 1990.

73. Jaynes, Julian, *The Origin of Consciousness in the Breakdown of the Bicameral Mind,* Boston, 1976.

74. Jong, J. de, *Le Labyrinthe,* Paris, 1963.

75. Johnson, Stewart, *The Ancien City of Suzhou. Town Planning in the Sung Dynasty.*

76. Joyce, James, *Daedalus,* NRF, 1924; *Ulysses,* NRF, 1937.

77. Jung, Carl Gustav, *L'Ame et la vie,* Buchet-Chastel, 1963, 1985; *Les Racines de la conscience,* Buchet-Chastel, 1971, 1983.

78. Kerenyi, *Labyrinthe Studien,* 2e éd., Zurich, Rhein Verlag, 1950.

79. Kern, Hermann, *Labyrinthe,* Prestel Verlag, Munich, 1982.

80. Knight, W.F., *Cumean Gates,* Basil Blackwell, Londres, 1936.

81. Kraft, John, *The Goddess in the Labyrinth,* Abo Akademi, Suède, 1985.

82. Lacarrière, J., *L'Envol d'Icare,* Seghers, 1993.

83. Laing, Ronald D., *Knots,* Stock-Plus.

84. Lascault, Gilbert, *Boucles et noeuds,* Balland, 1981; *Architecture primitive,* Beaubourg, Catalogue de l'exposition de Choisy-le-Roi: "Dédale et Ariane," 1985.

85. Leclerc, S.; Perrault, C., *Le Labyrinthe de Versailles,* Imprimerie Royal, 1779.

86. Lhote, Jean-Marc, *Le Symbolisme des jeux,* Berg international, 1976.

87. Lonegren, Sig, *The Labyrinths, Traditional Myths and Modern Applications,* Dangles, 1991.

88. Male, Émile, *Religious Art in France of the Thirteenth Century,* A. Colin, 1948, 1986.

89. Mallet, Robert, *Jardins et paradis,* Gallimard, 1959.

90. Marshack, Alexander, *The Roots of Civilization,* New York, 1972.

91. Matthews, W.H., *Mazes and Labyrinths,* Longmans Green, Londres, 1922.

92. Matthews, W.H., *Mazes and Labyrinths: their history and development,* New York, 1970.

93. Morrison, Tony, *The Mystery of the Nasca Lines,* Nonesuch Expeditions, 1987.

94. Nachman de Breslau, Rabbi, *La Chaise vide,* La Table Ronde, 1996.

95. Neitzsche, Freidrich, *Ariane à Naxos.*

96. Ovide, *The Metamorphoses,* Paris, Flammarion, 1966.

97. Pasquier, Gilles, *L'Entrée du labyrinthe,* Dervy, 1992.

98. Pennick, Nigel, *Labyrinths: their geomancy and symbolism,* Runestaff, 1986; *Mazes and Labyrinths,* Londres, 1990.

99. Philibert, Myriam, *La Naissance du symbole. Les racines du sacré,* Dangles, 1991.

100. Pieper, Jan, *Das Labyrintische,* Bibliothèque nationale.

101. Pline L'Ancien, *Histoire naturelle,* Paris, Belles lettres.

102. Plutarque, *Vie de Thésée,* Paris, Belles lettres, 1957.

103. Popper, Karl, *The Uncertain Universe: A Plea for Indeterminism,* Hermann, 1984.

104. Purce, Jill, *The Mystic Spiral: A Voyage of the Soul,* Paris, 1974.

105. Quéaux, Philippe, *Le Virtuel, vertus et vertiges,* "Milieux," INA, Paris, 1993.

106. Ragon, Michel, *L'Homme et les villes,* Albin Michel, 1975.

107. Ranchin, France de, *Labyrinthes,* Hatier, 1983; *Les Nouveaux Labyrinthes,* Höebeke, 1989.

108. Ravetz, Alison, *Deliverance and Disciplines. Review of Recent Works on Vandalism.*

109. Reed Dobb, Penelope, *L'Idée du labyrinthe de l'Antiquité au Moyen Age,* Cornell University Press, New York, 1990.

110. Robbe-Grillet, Alain, *Dans le labyrinthe,* Minuit, 1959.

111. Robinson, James M., *The Nag Hammadi Library,* San Francisco, 1977.

112. Rossel, André, *Labyrinthes, 18 jeux du temps passé,* Paris, 1968.

113. Saint-Hilaire, Paul de, *L'Univers secret du labyrinthe,* Robert Laffont, 1992.

114. Santarcangeli, Paolo, *The Book of Labyrinths,* Gallimard, 1974.

115. Sénèque, *Lettres à Lucilius (1-29),* Flammarion, Paris, 1992.

116. Serres, Michel, *La Naissance de la physique dans le texte de Lucrèce: fleuves et turbulences,* Minuit, 1977.

117. Shakespeare, William, *A Midsummer Night's Dream,* Belles Lettres, 1990.

118. Soyez, Edmond, *Les Labyrinthes d'église,* Yvert et Tellier, 1896.

119. Steinsaltz, Adin, *Le Maitre de prière,* Albin Michel, 1994.

120. Stern, Thomas, *Thésée ou la puissance du spectre,* Seghers, 1981.

121. Taylor, Mark C., *Errance. Lecture de Jacques Derrida,* Cerf, 1985.

122. Thibaud, Robert-Jacques, *Le Jeu de l'oie,* Dervy, 1995.

123. Trungpa, Chögyam, *Shambhala,* Seuil, 1990.

124. Turner, A.J., *The Time Museum,* Rockford, 1984.

125. Utudjian, Édouard, *L'Urbanisme souterrain,* PUF, Que sais-je?, 1952.

126. Van Zuylen, Gabrielle, *Tous les jardins du monde,* Découvertes Gallimard, 1994.

127. Viollet-Le-Duc, *Dictionnaire raisonné de l'architecture française,* "Labyrinthe," t. VI.

128. Virgile, *énéide,* Gallimard, 1974.

129. Waters, Franck, *The Book of the Hopi,* Nuage Rouge, Le Rocher, 1992.

130. Weiller, Danièle; Boyer, Michel-Antoine, *La Dimension urbaine,* Vincent.

131. Yates, Frances, *The Art of Memory,* Gallimard, 1966.

132. Zolbrod, Paul, *Le Livre des indiens Navajos,* Le Rocher, 1992.

Author References

133. *Archéologia,* juin 1969, "Un bien curieux monument, le labyrinthe d'église," R.P. A.-R. Vergrugghe.

134. Cohen, Daniel: from a conversation with the author.

135. *Ar'Site,* juin 1996.

136. *L'Histoire mystérieuse,* "Un voyage intérieur. Spirales et labyrinthes," juillet 1993.

137. *Chemins de France et pèlerinages,* n. 1.

138. *Revue d'Esthétique,* "Entrelacs et labyrinthe chez Vinci," Brion, Marcel, vol. 1, janv.-mars 1952.

139. Catalogue de l'Exposition à Choisy-le-Roi, *Dédale et Ariane,* 1985, Bibliothèque nationale.

140. Feraud, Jacqueline, *Jeu de l'oie, le fil d'Ariane ou jouer le jeu pour vivre le mythe,* Bibliothèque nationale.

141. Faure, Paul, "Dans le Labyrinthe," *L'Histoire* n. 197, mars 1996.